Michael Ho

HADRIAN AND ANTINOUS

THEIR LIVES AND TIMES

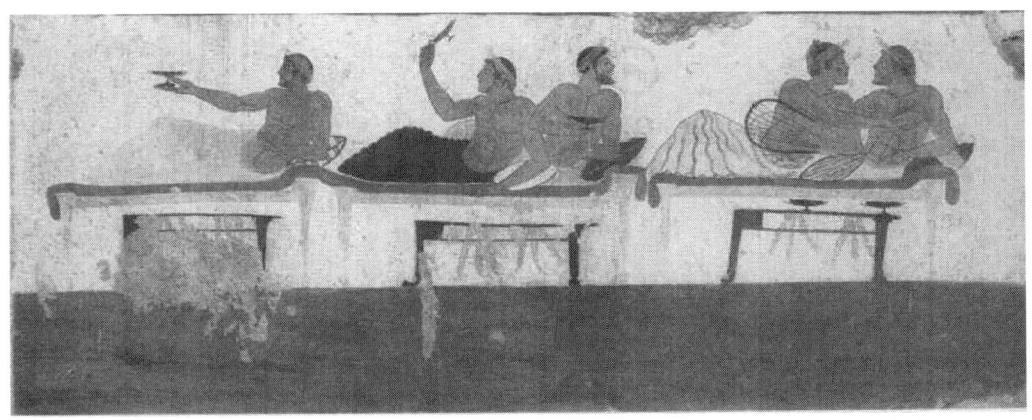

Hadrian favored Greek-style couches, the ultimate felicity.

Enlarged and Revised Edition
© 2018

"The boy was said to have fallen into the Nile, or, in truth, to have been offered as a human sacrifice. While still young Hadrian had fallen under the spell of soothsayers, fortunetellers, astronomers, augurs and the like and was willing to try all sorts of new spells and incantations. Perhaps he did so to bestow immortality on his belovèd, or perhaps to accomplish the ends he himself had in mind. What Hadrian did he did for love, or because the boy had voluntarily undertaken the ultimate sacrifice for him."
Cassius Dio

"Hadrian had wished to extend his lifespan by any means and had found the answer in charlatans who promised him immortality if a boy of supreme beauty would sacrifice himself, in the Nile, the source of immortality since the drowning of Osiris."
Aurelius Victor

Hadrian wondered at the enigma of humanity:
"Why did one mourn death--which was but eternal sleep-- and not the coming of age, which was the veritable human night?"

My books include: *Cellini, Caravaggio, Cesare Borgia, Renaissance Murders, TROY, Greek Homosexuality, ARGO, Alcibiades the Schoolboy, RENT BOYS, Buckingham, Homoerotic Art (in full color), Sailors and Homosexuality, The Essence of Being Gay, John (Jack) Nicholson, THE SACRED BAND, German Homosexuality, Gay Genius, SPARTA, Charles XII of Sweden, Mediterranean Homosexual Pleasure, CAPRI, Boarding School Homosexuality, American Homosexual Giants, HUSTLERS* and *Christ has his John, I have my George: The History of British Homosexuality*. I live in the South of France.

CONTENTS

BOOK ONE

Introduction
Page 5

Chapter One
≈ Inheritance ≈ Literature ≈ Daily Life and First Stirrings ≈ Philosophy and Superstition ≈
Page 7

Chapter Two
≈ Trajan at last Emperor ≈ The Dacian Wars ≈ Hadrian positions himself as Trajan's successor ≈
Page 16

Chapter Three
≈ Hannibal ≈ Scipio and Carthage ≈ The Punic Wars ≈
Page 31

Chapter Four
≈ Hadrian Emperor ≈ Proscription ≈ Mithridates ≈
Page 40

BOOK TWO

Chapter Five
≈ Roman Virility and Greek Love of Boys ≈
≈ Part 1 ≈
Page 49

Chapter Six
≈ The Boy ≈
Page 56

Chapter Seven
≈ Tibur ≈
Page 63

Chapter Eight
≈ Roman Virility and Greek Love of Boys ≈
≈ Part 2 ≈
Page 68

Chapter Nine
≈ The Boy's World: Sects, Religion, Astronomy, Superstition and Human Sacrifice ≈
Page 86

Chapter Ten
≈ The Boy's Deification ≈
Page 91

Chapter Eleven
≈ The Aftermath ≈
Page 101

Chapter Twelve
≈ Hadrian's Successors ≈
Page 107
≈ Hadrian's Deification ≈
Page 112

Sources
Page 115

Index
Page 128

≈≈

BOOK ONE

INTRODUCTION

The moving story of Hadrian and Antinous has spanned the ages not only as the bond of two men's love, but equally as an eternal mystery as to why a youth forfeited his life to perpetuate that of his lover. The enigma enveloping the account is an intensely personal one for me: During a trip to Athens I had shown sculptures of the head of Antinous to the boy who accompanied me, heads that were as identical to his own as two peas in a pod. I promised him that I would relate the story of Antinous' love for the emperor, which I did that night at a restaurant overlooking the Parthenon. The end of the story brought tears to his eyes, and tears to mine, because it was my telling of their love that had aroused his emotions. Several weeks later he too would be dead, in exactly the same way as Antinous, the precise account of which I've detailed in my autobiography (1).

This book is a historical work, historically correct. Naturally most of the book concerns Hadrian because we know far more about him than we do about the Bithynian Greek youth. There is also a heavy emphasis on the times in which they lived and the times that preceded them, as they played indelible roles in the two men's lives: indeed, they molded them.

Hadrian sought to quell his sexual needs through hunting and travel, through intellectual pursuits that made him knowledgeable in government, military affairs, architecture, philosophy and mysticism. He wanted to live forever and perhaps felt he possessed the intellectual and financial means to achieve that goal. He reminds me of a modern-day Richard Branson: can one imagine, for a second, that he is not exploring every means, possible or impossible, to extend his own lifespan? Such a man was Hadrian too, and such a quest very possibly led to the sacrifice of Antinous.

The book is a voyage that will take us into Roman and Greek daily life and, especially, daily sexuality; we'll review Hadrian's obsession with the occult and the importance of Egyptian Isis and Osiris in the death of Antinous; we'll go to Pontus to study the mass murderer Mithridates and then a little to the south, home of the Assassins and cutthroat cults like the Zealots and the Sicarii; we'll investigate the difference between male-male relations in Rome and the love of men for boys in Greece, the source of Antinous' sexuality; and, finally, we'll learn why Antinous drowned and why he become, for the first time in history, the only male companion to be deified, which not even Alexander the Great had been able to bestow on his beloved Hephaestion, despite the might of his armies.

Marriage was expected of a Roman citizen, a necessity since Spartan times when young men were obliged to produce the sons who would one day rise to salute them, as they now rose to salute their generals. Rome was forever on war footing, and men were increasingly needed in increasingly large numbers to furnish officers who would later take positions in governing the empire (if they survived, as the officers led their men in battle and were among the first to fall). Trajan, the emperor who took Hadrian into his home and who adopted him at the very end of his reign, married the intelligent and socially graceful Pompeia Plotina, a substitute mother for Hadrian, who interested the boy in literature, the arts and court decorum, as well as philosophies and the occult. Hadrian also eventually married, a woman he most probably never ''honored'', as Platina had most likely been left virginal by Trajan. So when Hadrian adopted Antonius Pius to succeed him, one historian half-jokingly remarked, ''at last, a man whose preference is women!''

The ancient world was a man's world, as is ours, and *Hadrian and Antinous* is, at its base, the story of that hallowed time when men were free to live their preference for other men.

CHAPTER ONE

≈ Inheritance ≈ Literature ≈ Daily Life and First Stirrings ≈
Philosophy and Superstition ≈

Publius Aelius Hadrianus Afer, called Hadrian, was born in 76 AD in either Rome or Italica, near today's Seville. The lack of exactitude signifies that his family was part of what the ancient aristocrats called ''new men'', rich thanks to Spanish lands but relatively unknown, and certainly not marked for future emperorship, since being born in Rome was far more advantageous for the careers of ''new men'' than being born in a hicksville such as Italica. As with all the gentry who shunned the strong possibility of having their child taken from them by dysentery or other maladies, his mother, Domitia Paulina, farmed him out to a wet-nurse, in Hadrian's case a healthy peasant, Germana, who would outlive her charge and played a role, later, in protecting his intimacy until his last breath. At age ten his father died, always a traumatic experience for a boy, leaving him very wealthy. He became ward of a cousin, Trajan, a native too of Italica, a soldier with a marked preference for boys, who also appreciated mountaineering, a man who married a virtuous wife, Plotina, leaving her, according to the busy-bodies of the time, as untouched as the Vestal Virgins. Later on Hadrian would choose a wife as immaculate, taking equal care to maintain her purity, although, unlike Plotina, she later took lovers (or so it was reported by chroniclers: the first was a saint, the second a slut). Hadrian's schooling consisted of as much math as necessary to function in the market, as well as rhetoric, syntax and literature based on Latin and Greek. Hadrian's heroes were Homer, of course, and Cicero, Cato, Coelius Antipater, Horace and Virgil, with a strong preference for Xenophon (see Sources). His philhellenism was his hallmark, and Aristotle, Socrates, Plato, Euripides and Aristophanes were intellectually intimate friends. His learning followed the Greek sophist tradition, sophists being teachers who specialized in teaching philosophy, rhetoric, music, athletics and mathematics, and he may have studied under Quintus Terentius Scaurus, an expert in grammar, noted for his commentaries on Homer and Virgil. Hadrian appreciated Greek more than Latin, and was said to have been more fluent in the language of Pericles. For him Greek culture was synonymous to intellectual glamor, earning him the nickname *Graeculus*, little Greek.

Hadrian
76 – 138 AD

In the ancient world puberty set in between ages 14 to 16, although James Davidson, in his "The Great Puberty Shift", claims that puberty began at age 18. During the Renaissance, fathers and select friends watched their sons consummate their marriages. The boys were usually around age 15, and even at that later time (compared to today) some had insufficient testosterone to fuel the lust needed to perform. The bedding of Catherine of Aragon by the brother of Henry VIII had not been observed, and when he soon died Catherine claimed he had been to weak to perform. Henry VIII married her and later asked for an annulment, claiming she had not been a virgin. The refusal of Pope Julius II to accord the separation led to the destruction of the Catholic Church in England, and thousands of deaths.

It was at puberty that Hadrian exchanged the purple-edged toga of a boy for the pure-white *toga virilis* of a man (*vir* meaning manly in Latin). As the best description of the ritual comes to us thanks to Ceasar's puberty, we will refer to it here: At age 15 Caesar exchanged the *toga praetexta* with its purple fringe for the pure white *toga virilis*. He was now a recognized citizen of Rome, responsible, in case of his father's death, for his mother and sisters and younger brothers. In Caesar's case, he had become the paterfamilias. He also put aside his *bulla praetexta*, a charm of gold held in a leather sack that parents put around their boy's neck, at age 9 days (time to see if he lived through the unsanitary conditions of childbirth), aimed at warding off evil spirits. The bulla, along with a lock of the boy's hair or, if the boy could, the first shavings from his chin, were placed on the family altar and dedicated to the Lares, guardian deities of the household. Mothers recuperated the bulla to protect the boy as he grew, to protect him especially from envious people who might wish him harm.

The ceremony was under the aegis of the god Liber. Liber means "the free one", the god of wine, fertility and freedom, the homegrown version of Bacchus/Dionysus. Liber accompanied a boy from puberty, from, specifically, his first orgasm, after which he exchanged the *toga praetexta* for the *toga virilis*. Liber was a phallic god, opposed to any form of servitude.

The ceremony took place in the Forum, surrounded by statues of Augustus and other Roman statesmen and generals, all of which represented a lad's obligation to filial duty, service to the state and commitment to serve his country militarily. From then on he would use his first name, his *praenomen*, in Hadrian's case Publius.

Roman boys and men were allowed male-slave-sexual-partners as a way of discharging their lust, an alternative form to pleasuring oneself. The male-slave-sexual-partner was generally replaced, sooner or later, by a wife. The slave would then cut his hair short and join the domain of the other household slaves.

By then Hadrian was certainly no longer pure. Sexual stimulation was all around him, furtive caresses as he passed through the streets and the corridors of the baths, looks and gestures of admirers who often paid boys' tutors for surreptitious introductions, down to the classroom itself where, as the poet Juvenal wrote,

> Boys played dirty games,
> Taking turns with one another,
> Trying not to be caught,
> While hands feverishly jerked,
> Until they came.

At home Hadrian had the continual spectacle of Trajan, his guardian, in delightful and casual interplay with the household youths, especially the handsome pages he was said to be infatuated with. Later, when Trajan became emperor, Hadrian knew instinctively that he could gain influence through the men important to Trajan by servicing them sexually, plowing through their bellies. In Rome sex was considered supremely natural (as it is there today). There were only a few rules to follow, which I'll get to later, but when a man was randy he satisfied himself with a passing slave, be it a him or a her.

In the same way that religion evolved over the millenniums as an antidote for man's inability to understand illness, death, madness, et al., so too evolved, concomitantly, magic, superstition and astrology, arms to help men compensate for their ignorance. Hadrian too fell victim to such concepts, the result of which would have terrible consequences in his interactions with Antinous, a boy as removed from the black arts as Hadrian was close. Trajan's wife Plotina was known to have had immense influence on her husband and the very young Hadrian. She followed the teachings of Epicurus, a philosophy known as Epicureanism, devoted to having pleasure while avoiding pain. Death was the end of the body and soul and thusly should not be awed. As the gods were indifferent to men, they should be ignored. The ideal Epicurean sought a tranquil family life, simple and without tribulation, although Hadrian's life was filled with much too much movement and activity for him to know simplicity and calm. Only the emperor Augustus had been able to do so, but then, he was a god. Another philosophy found in Rome was Stoicism, named after *stoa*, the Greek colonnades that surrounded the Agora in Athens. Since the cosmos ruled the fates of men, and men would be eternally too unknowledgeable to understand the cosmos, one had to accept one's fate willingly, whatever it was. This acceptance applied to death which a man had to face in a manly manner, seeing that forfeiting one's life was only giving back what henceforth belonged to another.

Every powerful Roman had his clients and was known to them as their protector. The protector provided food, money and judicial help (should a client need it) in exchange for the client's vote on issues important to the protector, as well as various small services. The clients met at the protector's home in the morning and accompanied him to the Forum. Hadrian's father had had clients, and as they were handed down from one generation to another, they were now his. The streets the protector and the clients wandered through were not exclusively bordered by gardens, fountains and public baths. Most were narrow and dirty, and the noise, especially at night when drovers cursed their horses and oxen as they rattled over cobblestones, kept Romans from sleep. The byways stank from the nearby abattoir and the buildings, poorly constructed, could, at any moment, come tumbling down. As there was no lighting at night, men unaccompanied by guards faced being beaten and robbed. Squares lit by torches and open fires were frequented by whores and rent-boys showing off their wares (just like today, on roads leading to and out of Rome, Fellinian and Pasolinien extravaganzas). Politics were discussed at the Forum, but with the advent of Augustus all power was now in the hands of the emperor, so that the Consuls, the Senate and the Tribunes, all of which had been of vital importance to a republic, were maintained only to perpetuate the illusion of republicanism. The emperor's word was law because the people had made him sovereign.

There were many people of Spanish origin among Hadrian's clients. His father Aelius Hadrianus Afer had been born in Spain, as had his mother, Domitia Paulina, born near today's Cadiz (ancient Gades). His father had been a senator, a man of wealth, and in Rome the family lived in a quarter of the city where a great number of citizens of Spanish descent resided, and perhaps even a fourth of the Senate was comprised of men of Spanish origin. It was Emperor Claudius who had given trans-Alpines the right to serve as magistrates and senators, and Vespasian and his son Titus who bestowed patrician status on provincials, which admitted them into the ruling classes. Soon the families of Trajan and Hadrian, born near or around Italica (itself eight miles from today's Seville) no longer even spoke Spanish. When they migrated to Rome they came with the wealth of the Spanish lands they still held, lands rich in gold, silver, copper and vital olive oil, needed for cooking and fuel, taking the place of soap when applied to the skin and then scraped off with strigils.

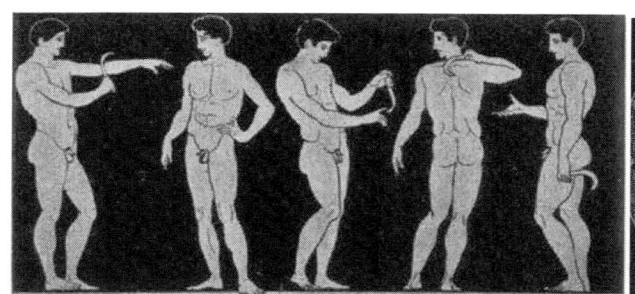

Athletes using a strigil.

To the outside world Romans sought to perpetuate themselves through war, the tribute from which could produce, on occasion, a tidal wave of wealth in the form of foodstuffs, gold, silver, slaves and other booty. In the same way that civilization today is at times compared to a virus that maintains itself by destroying the lives of others, Romans too were known for rape, butchery and plunder, sparing neither the poor nor the rich--the rich whose estates the emperors could pillage for their own benefit. Romans were often considered uncouth, only good for appropriating the gods, literature, dress and eating manners of the Greeks. They appropriated too the Greek love of boys. Every Roman was aware that Apollo had been the first god to initiate night games among boys. Apollo's favorite was Hyacinth whom the West Wind had killed by blowing back a discus the boy had thrown, shattering his skull, in reprisal for Hyacinth having spurned his advances. Zeus, attracted by his son's wailing over the lifeless corpse, wondered how boy-love could bring on such a reaction. He found out when he abducted the Trojan youth Ganymede for his bed and--to ward off smirks--dissimulated the fact by making him his cupbearer. Soon Man followed suit. The Spartans made boy-love a virile pursuit in which lovers became valorous warriors, preferring death to the betrayal of the boys they loved. The Athenians turned boy-love into a philosophical pastime in which, thanks to Eros, the intellectual and the physical were joined to make a new, self-sufficient man. In time the Trojan Aeneas took the custom to the city he was destined to found on the banks of the Tiber. But this would be neither the virile love of hasty couplings known to the Spartans, nor intellectual fusion of body and soul practiced by Athenians, but a monstrous, degenerative debauch of painted faces, effeminate bodies and fat slavering perverts, the world of *Satyricon* and Tiberius.

In some quarters there was a significant backlash against the Greeks, Romans tired of hearing that what they possessed best was of Greek origin, even their way of thinking and debating. The poet Juvenal (see Sources) satirically wrote that Greeks were quick-witted, shamelessly bold and glib, chameleons who could turn themselves into anything in order to gain position and wealth, becoming teachers or painters or grammarians, musicians, doctors or, why not?, tightrope walkers and magicians?

An event that molded the world in which Hadrian was born was the destruction of the Temple in Jerusalem and the mass suicides of Jews on the high plateau of Masada. To escape from being taken for a Jew, many men in Greece, where games and gymnastics were performed nude, tried to recover their lost foreskins either by operations, the result of which often ended in death through infection, or by wearing weights around the prepuce, thereby stretching the skin over the glans, hopefully permanently (2). An uncovered glans was considered unsightly by the Greeks and some boys tied their foreskins shut to prevent its accidental display. Another major event, similar to the sudden arrival of Sputnik for us, was the eruption of Vesuvius that Pliny the Younger (see Sources) described as heralding the end of the world.

With the death of Nero, Augustan rule was replaced by Flavian rule (most Flavians had Flavius as a middle name), under which Hadrian passed much of his early life. Vespasian became emperor thanks to his generalship over 80,000 men. He was heralded for building the Coliseum and public urinals, known today as Vespasians in some parts of the world. The urinals were taxed because urine was collected for bleaching fabrics, and when Vespasian was criticized for this he answered that money gained from urinals, unlike urine, had no odor and was therefore acceptable. At his death, knowing that he would be deified, he said: "My goodness, I'm becoming a god!" His oldest son Titus took his place but soon died of fever. Domitian succeeded Titus. He restored laws against sexual congress between men (the word homosexual was still hundreds of years from being coined), although he was known to appreciate rough sex with boys and girls, girls apparently the center of his interests.

At age nineteen Hadrian took on small public positions, thanks to help from his guardian, Trajan. He was named to the Board of Ten whose purpose was to decide cases involving civil disputes. At the time the Roman state had no public prosecutors, nor did it have a police force or even jails, as such. But men with oratorical skills sprang up to defend or to prosecute the accused, and as the Romans loved oratory, these cases attracted crowds and instant popularity to men with speaking ability, men who became known as lawyers. These men, these advocates, gained great wealth and either good or reprehensible reputations. Delators brought charges against citizens, and if they won in court they would gain part of the penalties; if they lost, however, the delators became subject to the same penalties as those of the accused.

Under Domitian, Hadrian was put in charge of organizing several yearly festivals consisting of chariot racing, gymnastics, poetry reading and singing, as well as footraces for girls. The origin of gladiatorial games is lost in time, but Pliny states they started during the First Punic War. Some believe they were combats at the funerals of important men, a form of human sacrifice that was found in many parts of the world, usually implicating women who voluntarily (or not) followed their husbands into the afterworld. During a period of 123 days Trajan, to celebrate his victory over the Dacians (more later), called upon 10,000 gladiators. It is estimated that perhaps 4,000 gladiators were killed annually, one in six per performance. Gladiators were the last word in masculinity, but ceased to exist due to the increasingly prohibitive cost of their services (as well as the advent of Christianity which considered the games no more than legalized murder). The gladiatorial combats were highly sensual affairs. Prostitutes lined the ways leading from the coliseum where the killing of men--the sight and smell of blood--raised the sexual excitement of the spectators to red-hot levels, their erections an acknowledgement of being alive, so unlike the bodies strewn over the sand in the arena, the vital need of orgasm now, right now, pushed them to seek out the women waiting outside. The prostitutes earned their money, for the men and their brutal thrusts were the mirror image of the gladiatorial spectacle they had just left, only here each was armed with the drive of his blood-engorged phallus, the equivalent of the gladiator's bloodstained sword.

Trajan dispatched Hadrian to Pannonia, today's Hungry, as governor, where he commanded the Legion II Adiutrix, the same legion in which he had begun his military career. The Roman army was divided into legions of about 5,000 men, which in turn were divided into ten cohorts. There were 6 centurions per cohort, and within each cohort were tents of 8 men who became tighter than brothers, never hesitating to die for their companions. The soldiers had good food and medical care, were paid on time (1,400 sesterces a year of a private, at the very least 18,000 for a centurion). They couldn't marry but had mistresses and often children they legitimized when they left the service. The governor of Pannonia just happened to be Trajan. Hadrian learned the proper way to treat soldiers from Trajan, who ate with his men what they ate, traveled with them on foot, led them in dirty songs and, in general, suffered when they suffered. Also like Trajan, Hadrian had a near-perfect memory for names. Beyond Pannonia was Dacia, an unknown land thanks to which Trajan would eventually become emperor.

CHAPTER TWO

≈ Trajan at last Emperor ≈ The Dacian Wars ≈ Hadrian positions himself as Trajan's successor ≈

We know that Hadrian was devoted to the hunt from his earliest years, something which did not necessarily please Trajan as hunting was not considered a noble pastime by the ruling classes. This did not dissuade Hadrian who perhaps knew of the Greek Xenophon's opinion on the subject: ''The hunt is the best training for war, and keeps the body healthy, improves a lad's sight and hearing, and helps him prolong his youth.'' Xenophon was Hadrian's hero, a man he preferred to Homer, perhaps in part because, as said, Xenophon favored love between men and boys, a subject Homer avoided.

Xenophon was not only a general of genius, a valiant hero who fought for Cyrus the Younger during his youth, the stirring adventure that is the heart of his *Anabasis*, he was in addition a philosopher, historian, the author of *Hellenica*, the story of the Peloponnesian War. Born in Athens but an admirer of Sparta where he sent his sons to be trained, this man among men galvanized his followers thanks to his courage, protection, guidance and his first priority, their education, the ultimate for those that seek a model who exemplifies the belief that true good, profound inspiration, the very finest in what mankind can offer, come through a lover's will to better the boy who so tenderly, gratefully, willingly, fills his bed with his perishable warmth.

A pupil of Socrates, he believed in rule by the best, the closest model of which he found in Sparta. His prose is as straightforward as the man himself, the reason he was and is studied by students of Greek culture, history, philosophy and language. The simplicity and extensiveness of his oeuvre is such that he was known as the Attic Muse.

Born around 430 BC, Xenophon left for Persia with his lover Proxenus where he spent a great deal of time alongside Cyrus the Younger, the son of Darius. Cyrus had become very friendly with the Spartan Lysander, convinced that Lysander was the only honest man he'd ever met. When Darius became ill, Cyrus, astonishingly, turned over his governorship to Lysander, while he went to his father's deathbed in Susa. But his brother Artaxerxes, not Cyrus, was named king, and Cyrus attempted to assassinate him. He failed although he was pardoned, always a mistake. Instead of thanking Artaxerxes for sparing his life, Cyrus the Younger raised an army, among whom were Xenophon's 10,000 (all of which is the subject of *Anabasis*). Cyrus the Younger met his brother in combat where Cyrus was killed. According to Plutarch (see Sources), the boy was killed by a soldier named Mithridates who struck him with a blow that felled him from his horse. Cyrus' head was cut off by Artaxerxes' eunuch, Masabates. Cyrus' mother had Mithridates captured and killed by scaphism, the ancient Persian way: The victim was stripped naked and placed between two rowboats that closed one on the other like a walnut, with only the head and arms and legs protruding. He was then fed milk and honey that caused a diarrhea that filled the interior space and attracted insects which would eat and breed in the man's flesh until nothing remained but bone. Later she won Masabates, the eunuch, in a game of dice and had him flayed alive. After Cyrus' death Xenophon and his ten thousand made their way back home, the breathtaking account of which ends his *Anabasis*.

The Athenians exiled him when he fought with the Spartans against Athens but the Spartans offered him an estate where he wrote his works. Most of what we know about Sparta today we know thanks to Xenophon, as the Spartans seem to have limited themselves to warfare, not historical literature.

Xenophon's *Apology* details the life, trial and forced suicide of Socrates. Plato claimed that Socrates used his trial as a means of educating the Athenians as to the moral issues behind his accusations, thusly coming off as arrogant. Xenophon maintains that Socrates did so because he wanted to be found guilty, knowing that his death would lead them to the indelible conclusion that all men should be free to express their opinions. Despite Socrates' end, we nonetheless have the Athenian way of life to thank for the ascension of these three men who have shaped the minds of free men to our very day, Xenophon, Socrates and Plato, a heritage Hadrian made his own.

In Xenophon's works he related stories of love that Hadrian would have known and certainly appreciated:

The first concerns Cyrus the Younger. Cyrus was going away on travels and the custom was that he kiss his relatives on the mouth. A certain lad, in love with Cyrus and wanting to be kissed too, told him that he was a distant member of his family. Cyrus said that he had noticed the lad because he never took his eyes off him. The boy blushed and said that he hadn't dared introduce himself. Cyrus conceded that as he was a relative, he too deserved a kiss, which he gave him. The boy stated that as he was going off on an adventure, and since Persians kissed during such times, he merited a second kiss. Cyrus laughed and bestowed it. The boy rode away but rapidly returned, his horse in a lather. ''Is it not true,'' the boy asked, ''that when one returns after a time one is received with a kiss?'' ''You weren't away long enough,'' smiled Cyrus. ''How can you say that when being away from someone as beautiful as you, for even a second, is like a year?'' Cyrus grinned and told the boy he would soon join him and that from then on he wouldn't be absent for even a second.

Xenophon goes on to describe a tender battle scene in which a certain Episthenes, seeing that a handsome enemy boy was about to be executed, ran to Xenophon and begged for the boy's life. Xenophon approached his general, Seuthes, in charge of Episthenes, to ask if the lad's life could be spared, as Episthenes had shown himself a valiant warrior. Seuthes asked Episthenes if he would be willing to take the boy's place and be executed. Episthenes stretched out his neck and told Seuthes to strike off his head if the boy so ordered. The boy came forward to save Episthenes, but dropped to his knees and begged that both their lives be spared. Episthenes rose and enfolded the lad in his arms, telling Seuthes that he would have to kill them or let them both go free. Seuthes laughed and, says Xenophon, winked at him. The story is certainly true, for someone of Xenophon's value would never have recounted it otherwise.

Sometime during this period Hadrian returned to Italica for a visit, and later honored the home of his birth with new temples, baths and an amphitheater, improvements not destined to last as the town was abandoned and wheat was said to have been grown in the amphitheater, just as in Rome during the time of the first popes, when sheep grazed in what had been the Imperial Forum.

Domitian had made enemies, among them a servant, Stephanus, upset because the emperor had killed his secretary, a friend of Stephanus. Others were involved, perhaps even Nerva who may have been forewarned and promised the emperor's place. Stephanus had feigned an injury allowing him to wear bandages, under which he hid a knife. He had also removed a sword that Domitian kept under his pillow. An astrological prediction had warned the emperor that he would die that day at noon, the reason why he repeatedly asked Stephanus the time. The servant lied, saying it was now well passed noon, and counseled the emperor to relax. As Domitian took up writing, Stephanus bent over him and, say the ancient sources with unexpected precision, stabbed him in the groin. A struggle ensued during which Domitian killed Stephanus but was himself knifed multiple times by conspirators who came rushing to help the servant when they heard the emperor cry out.

Domitian had been the third of the Flavian emperors, the first his father Vespasian, the second his brother Titus. So hated was Domitian's reign, so tyrannical, that at his death the Senate condemned him to oblivion, while authors at the time, Tacitus, Pliny the Younger and Suetonius (see Sources), followed suit by relating his despotism and cruelty. Yet his tireless efforts to strengthen the Roman economy, his defense of imperial borders and his massive building projects, set Rome squarely on the road to stability and one of the longest periods of relative peace in its history.

Domitian was said to have been handsome in his youth, and like Caesar he detested his baldness, that he covered with wigs, and even wrote a book on hair care. Such was the hostility of historians that one can be certain of few facts concerning him, especially those claiming he wanted control over private and public morals, and was ferociously against male-male relations, while preferring his sex, with both genders, rough.

Historians wrote that his youth had been solitary and unsettling, solitary due to the loss of his mother and the perpetual absence of his father and brother off waging war, and unsettling because it came at the close of Nero's chaotic reign. His family came to power at the end of the Civil War in 69 AD, followed by the turmoil of the year of the Four Emperors, which saw the rise of Galba, Otho, Vitellius and, finally, his father Vespasian, thanks to the hold Vespasian had over Judaea and Egypt, commander of 80,000 men, while his brother Titus Flavius Sabinus II controlled the garrison of Rome. Domitian was taken prisoner at the time by Vitellius, and when he learned that his father's brother Sabinus was captured by Vitellius and murdered, his body thrown to the dogs, he disguised himself as a worshipper of Isis and escaped. The next day Vitellius himself was captured, cast down the Gemonian stairs and decapitated, along with his son and his brother.

At the death of Vespasian his son Titus took seamless control, the major event of his reign the eruption of Vesuvius in 79 AD, to which he dedicated himself to the coordination of relief efforts. He died of fever two years into his emperorship. Domitian was accused of murdering him, either directly or by letting him die unaided during his illness. Whatever the case, Domitian wasted no time in taking control, openly bypassing the Senate by establishing what he declared to be a divine monarchy. The solitary young man now ruled solitarily, but even his enemy Suetonius admitted that his running of the government was excellent. He ordered adultery penalized by exile, and libelous writings, especially against himself, punished by exile or death. Mimes were forbidden, ostensibly because of their use of obscene gestures, but more likely because they made fun of Domitian. As Vestal Virgins were daughters of Rome, having sex with them was a form of incest, punished by their being buried alive. He had his father and brother deified, along with his son, dead at age three.

Domitian reinforced the value of the denarius by increasing its silver content; the flipside celebrated the deification of his son.

Like Hadrian later on, Domitian refused to expand the Roman Empire's borders, and fought only when attacked, which was nonetheless often. He nevertheless expanded the Empire up to modern Scotland, but was forced to withdraw the troops for service in the Dacian Wars. Although it was Trajan who eventually ended the Wars, they began in 85 when Dacian King Decebalus crossed the Danube in an offensive invasion. Even though Decebalus killed a Roman governor and a Roman general, Domitian sued for peace when war broke out on the German border, one far more important in the defense of Rome than Dacia, and Decebalus was given 8 million sesterces annually to keep him at bay, a peace that sparked enormous unrest among Domitian's troops. Domitian may have wished to simply gain time before launching a new campaign against Decebalus, but he died too soon for us to know.

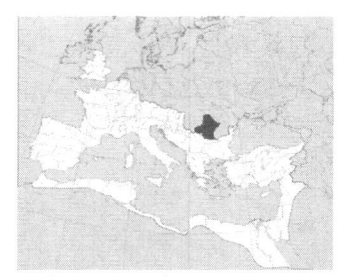

Dark area: Dacian territory annexed by Trajan.

After Domitian's assassination the Senate immediately passed *damnatio memoriae* on him, ordering the destruction of his coins, statues, arches and had his name excised from all public records. Suetonius stated that Romans in general were indifferent to his passing, but that he was grieved by the army which ordered his deification and the execution of his assassins, both demands denied by Domitian's successor, Marcus Cocceius Nerva, an unexpected repost since Nerva was sick, but one that led many to assume that Nerva himself had had a hand in the murder.

At any rate, for the first time in its history, the Senate voted in an emperor, Nerva, an important government official under Nero and the Flavians. Historians feel that the Senate acted with alacrity in order to stay civil war, and if Trajan had not been so far away he would have been easily nominated. Nerva was also a good administrator but nearly as unpopular as Domitian had been. He was not without ideas though, one of which was to take advantage of Trajan's recent victories over German tribes.

Hoping that Trajan's popularity would rub off on him, Nerva adopted Trajan in exactly the way Caesar had adopted Augustus, in effect informing the world that this was his choice of successor.

Hadrian instantly knew that his own time had come. He believed in the magic of numbers and knew the importance of 7. At the age of 7 a boy was deemed capable of reason. At 14 came puberty and at 21 he became a man, traditions we today more or less follow. Hadrian was now 21 and, he felt certain, on the threshold of a huge change in his life. Another multiple of 7, 63 (9 times 7), was feared by men because many died then. Emperor Augustus himself sighed with relief when he turned 64. And if proof was needed, Nerva, at 63, suddenly caught cold and breathed his last. The world had just as suddenly become an oyster, first for Trajan, assuredly next for Hadrian.

As Trajan was serving on the Rhine, Hadrian set out to be the first to bring him the news that he was now emperor. In this Hadrian had a rival, Trajan's brother-in-law Julius Servianus who set out at the same time, but not before sabotaging Hadrian's carriage. Hadrian nonetheless made it first and was rewarded by Trajan's decision to keep him near him. At a later date Hadrian considered Servianus as a probable successor, only to change his mind near the end of his reign. He then groomed Servianus' grandson Gnaeus Pedanius Fuscus for the role, something Servianus agreed to, notably because Servianus was now in his 90s. When Hadrian again changed his mind and designated someone else, Fuscus and Servianus decided to overthrow him, which led to their executions (although some historians believe Hadrian had them killed so they would not be alive to oppose his choice of emperor after his death).

Now that Hadrian was a heartbeat from power, he discovered that many of Trajan's influential friends and bedmates, through sheer jealousy, plotted his downfall. Luckily he had a sincere friend in Trajan's wife, Plotina. She gave him good counsel and helped choose his wife, Vibia Sabina, a wealthy, young heiress who never developed a liking for him, as he never did for her. Sexual penetration could be a ravaging experience for very young girls, a fate Vibia, 15, was apparently spared. Spared too, according to Sabina, was the human race, which she had saved, she later claimed, by not having a child with Hadrian, a claim that adds support to the likelihood that theirs had been a *marriage blanc*.

Hadrian followed Plotina's advice to be moderate in all things, and Trajan's example by being conciliate with senators, in whose body he entered at age 24, and by praising the army wherein resided the real power. Trajan nominated him for the important role of government spokesman, but he was laughed at because of his accent, proof that either he had been raised in Spain and not in Rome (remember that being born and raised in Rome, as many falsely claimed to have been, would favor a political career as he would be an "insider") or, as some believed, he had been influenced by the often-sloppy way of speaking favored by centurions and their troops, in whose midst he had spent much time. Others maintain that, as a Hellenist, he spoke much better Greek than he did Latin, while, finally, still others insist that all the talk about Hadrian having an accent of any sort was nonsense, and that he spoke Latin as well as any other Roman. Naturally, we'll never know.

Trajan may have encouraged Plotina to find a wife for Hadrian as a means of giving Hadrian other sexual outlets. Indeed, Hadrian was far too friendly with Trajan's pages, boys Trajan "loved immodestly" wrote P. Southern in his *The Roman Army, a Social and Institutional History*, 2007. The *Historia Augusta* (see Sources) recounts that Hadrian "cultivated Trajan's boy favorites and had often had sexual relations with them". The marriage didn't calm Hadrian sexually, as he was a virile 25, but as boys were available everywhere, Hadrian apparently decided to leave Trajan's favorites to Trajan, and sought companionship elsewhere. At any rate, tensions between the two lessened, which was in Hadrian's interests. That said, male-male relations in the army were forbidden, and transgressors were killed, often clubbed to death by their fellow soldiers, a form of hypocrisy in Caesar's time where outside Caesar's tent his soldiers ribbed him mercilessly, commenting on his having been King Nicomedes' lover (Nicomedes who was King of Bithynia, Antinous' birthplace), while warning girls to watch out for the baldheaded fucker. Caesar was a man to every woman and a woman to every man, yet so loved that someone was posted behind him in his chariot as he rode through Rome during the celebration of his Triumphs, who whispered into his ear while he was being wildly cheered, ''Remember, you are not a god''.

But the marriage to Libia Sabina did put Hadrian in ballpark vicinity to Trajan's family, certainly the main reason Hadrian didn't put up a fuss when the match was suggested, especially as Hadrian was well placed to see firsthand that Trajan would never sire children of his own.

Trajan initiated reforms, laws to protect minors and deserted children. Until then, Romans shared the Spartan tradition of abandoning children when they found them physically deficient, children rescued by childless couples or those who needed free labor. He also did away with the absolute power fathers had over their sons, power which allowed them to even put the youths to death. In one well-known case, involving a youth who did not manage the transition from sexually passive to active, his father, Quintus Fabius Maximus Eburnus, had his son killed for being ''unchaste''. The hypocrisy of the matter was that when Fabius himself was young he was called a ''chick'', signifying a boy-love-object, known for his good-looks and availability. His reaction towards his son was perhaps a counter-reaction against his own juvenile misdeeds. Trajan also initiated penalties against fathers who left all of their estates to only one son while neglecting the others.

Trajan and Plotina installed themselves on the Palatine Hill, a complex of luxurious residences of marble, frescoes and gardens that overlooked the racecourse, the Circus Maximus. The Circus Maximus was especially remembered as the site where Sulla gathered 9,000 prisoners and, in the presence of senators and the general public, he went over the fine points of his assuming ultimate power in Rome while down below the prisoners, screaming for mercy, had their throats slit or swords thrust into their chests, in sound and view of Sulla, the senators, Rome's nobility and everyone else.

The emperor could not immediately benefit from his new household as he was forced to go to Dacia, accompanied by Hadrian, where King Decebalus, previously mentioned, was again causing trouble. Dacia was a wild country, located in Transylvania and encircled by the Carpathian Mountains, the home of bats, wolves and mythical monsters. Dacians fought with curved machetes, a weapon that inspired more fear than simple swords and spears because of their disfiguring damage. Trajan welcomed the war against the Dacians because he knew that the best way to unite the nation was by bringing it together in defense of Rome's gates. The campaign was also an excellent opportunity for Hadrian to become still closer to Trajan, so Hadrian made certain that he was always in calling distance of the emperor, and always there to keep Trajan company while they drank themselves into a stupor.

There were two major incidents during the campaign. The first implicated a Roman that King Decebalus had turned. The Roman was sent to Trajan's camp for the purpose of murdering the emperor in full view of the troops, the first recorded incident of what we today call terrorism, a man sent on a suicide mission. Luckily the Roman was recognized by comrades and, after torture, admitted to King Decebalus' role in the aborted attempt. The second major incident involved the commander Cnaeus Pompeius Longinus (I rarely give full names, but in this case it's to honor the commander). He was lured to a peace conference with King Decebalus, but despite assurances that he would be safe, he was taken prisoner. The king sent word to Trajan that either the emperor grant the Dacians soft peace conditions or the young commander would be put to death. The commander, after bringing one of his jailors over to his cause, took poison the jailor smuggled to him, freeing Trajan from having to decide between submission or victory.

When all else failed, Decebalus had the river Sargetia diverted in order for slaves to dig a huge hole wherein they hid his treasure of gold and silver. The hole was covered with boulders and the river returned to its natural bed. Alas for the king, an informer revealed everything to Trajan's soldiers. The game up, Decebalus cut his own throat with the curved machete. Trajan's men completed the task by beheading him, Decebalus' head and right hand sent to the emperor. Those of the Dacrians not decimated by Trajan's troops, thousands of them, were dispersed throughout neighboring lands. Many became gladiators in order to survive.

Decebalus committing suicide, depicted on Trajan's column, and a 40-meter-high rock sculpture in his honor, as he is a national Romanian hero.

In 113 Trajan raised the famous, still-standing column to his Dacian victories, and offered Hadrian a diamond ring as a memento, a clear sign of Trajan's favor. The Dacian campaigns brought Rome immense wealth, said by one source to have equaled 700 tons of silver, as well as gold mines that became Roman when Dacia was absorbed into the empire.

Trajan's Column in celebration of his Dacian 101-102 and 105-106 AD victories. Trajan and his wife Plotina were buried at its base.

In addition to gladiatorial games in honor of his victories, Trajan authorized pantomime acts, shows that told a story through facial and bodily movements, shows that had been censored by Domitian and by Trajan too, as reported, because they were occasions of great obscenity, the ideal means of poking fun at emperors, but he later reversed himself, the reason for his revised decision perhaps being the pantomime actor Pylades, a boy the emperor had fallen in love with. Trajan decided to give a push to other boys too, and girls, by awarding them allocations, money most used for their education and physical training, assurance that the empire would continue to have intelligent and strong men for the running of the country and the army, and healthy, well-fed women to procreate.

Hadrian had expected Trajan to give him a push forward by adopting him, an act that was becoming a tradition thanks to Caesar's adoption of Augustus and Nerva's adoption of Trajan. But Trajan refused to do so. A disciple of Alexander the Great, Trajan felt, as did Alexander, that his succession should go ''to the fittest''. But Hadrian was chosen by the emperor to write his speeches, which prolonged the intimacy that had begun with the drinking bouts in Dacia. As an added gift Trajan named him archon of Athens, a kind of ruler, for the duration of the Panathenaic Games of 112. Hadrian oversaw athletic contests, competitions in poetry, music and rhetoric, along with the presentations of the plays by Aeschylus, Sophocles, Euripides and Aristophanes. Up until then Romans had been clean-shaven, a fashion started by Scipio Africanus (about whom we'll learn much more later). Only during war campaigns did men let their beards grow out. But the Greeks wore trimmed beards and Hadrian, the purest of philhellenes, followed suit.

Hadrian beardless and bearded. Hadrian copied the Greeks in adopting a beard, which he probably considered butch, a precursor of today's designer stubble.

In Athens he saw to the completion, then and during later visits, of the temple of Zeus, began by Peisistratus in the 6th century BC (4), and the building of a new aqueduct, a Pantheon and a library. He also took part in the Eleusinian Mysteries, as only Augustus had before him.

Back in Rome Trajan, perhaps through boredom, perhaps to stir the people, surely to gain wealth, surely too to make a greater name for himself, decided to go to war, choosing Parthians for his victims, a warrior people who occupied immense lands from today's Pakistan to the Euphrates. Expert horsemen, they used kohl to line their eyes and other make-up, and took great care with braiding their hair (Darius, in Oliver Stone's *Alexander*, is a perfect portrait of a Parthian). The excuse for the intervention was the Parthians' excessive interest in Armenia, considered by Rome to be in its sphere of influence. The reality was that the Parthians were far too busy warring among themselves to be a real threat to Armenia or anyone else, passing their time in civil strife or trying to decide which royal uncle, brother or son would be allowed to live long enough to gain power over fellow Parthians.

Hadrian was sent to Antioch, capital of Syria, to await the arrival of the emperor. He whiled away his time in the most sexually promiscuous city in the empire, where every woman opened her quiver to every arrow. He followed the adage that sexual pleasure came through changing sexual partners, and never lacked for company, often provided by fathers who sought influence by throwing their sons at him.

Trajan finally showed up and favored Hadrian by turning over command to him. Alas for Hadrian, the Parthians drew the Romans deep into their endless country, as the Russians would Napoleon and Hitler. The extended supply lines, weather of such heat and cold as to defy imagination, insects and dysentery (the ultimate decimator of armies throughout all history), led to a Roman defeat, even if Trajan refused to recognize it as one. He just left, airily maintaining that he had won, but not before an attack of diarrhea floored him (until the end he maintained that someone was poisoning him, as the great Augustus had purportedly been slowly poisoned by the wife he adored).

As Trajan's condition worsened, and the scourge of the battlefield, humiliating and filthy, finally did him in, he adopted Hadrian, age 41. Hadrian had been forewarned of his ascension by fortunetellers, a banal occurrence for the time but one that would give credence to Hadrian's belief in the occult, which would later lead him to Pachrates and other charlatans, perhaps responsible, later still, for Antinous' death. Immediately, Hadrian had a gold piece minted showing him on one side, with his new beard, and Trajan on the other, facing Plotina.

Hadrian along with Trajan facing Plotina.

Thusly the little boy from Italica, the little Greek, became the new emperor, and Trajan, deified, took his place in the Roman godhood.

CHAPTER THREE

≈ Hannibal ≈ Scipio and Carthage ≈ The Punic Wars ≈

Among the writers Hadrian appreciated most was the philhellenic Quintus Ennius, a writer who had personally known Scipio Africanus, Hannibal's nemesis. Hadrian was impassioned by the story of Hannibal because it was Roman history, which he adored, and because the events originated near his Spanish birthplace. In fact, Scipio himself had been born in Hadrian's native Italica. In another turn of fate, Hannibal found his death in Bithynia, birthplace of Antinous, and it was near Italica that Hamilcar Barca debarked to establish what became known as New Carthage.

Hannibal Barca
247 BC – C. 180 BC

All began with Aeneas, the son of a Trojan warrior and Aphrodite, who escaped Troy after its destruction by the Greeks, setting sail towards the western Mediterranean. On his way he stopped over at Carthage where he romanced Queen Dido, a Phoenician princess who had founded the city. Jilting her, Aeneas went on to found Rome, thereby sowing the seeds of future animosity between the two countries, mercantile Carthage and belligerent Rome.

Hera and Athena had inspired Aeneas' founding of Rome, as the extension of the curse responsible for the destruction of Troy:

> ''The survivors for years will roam the endless seas,
> Till coming to a western land of hills and trees.
> And there in pious memory of Troy of old,
> A mighty empire with naked hands will mold.
> But Hera and Athena's curse will waste their home;
> Into monstrous vice will descend eternal Rome.''

Rome and Carthage grew separately, the first becoming a military power made rich through conquest, the second gaining wealth through trade. Rome developed a unique attitude towards war: it would be total and Rome would never surrender. There would be no treaties until Rome had conquered its enemy, no matter how long such conquest took. The competition between generals for the best political positions in Rome, tribunals, senators, consuls and such was so ferocious that no general would risk the disapproval of his countrymen by accepting anything short of victory over an enemy. Rome's second asset (the first being all-out war) was its ability to incorporate subjected countries, sending Roman citizens to colonize them as well as accepting native populations into the Roman flock, thanks to which Rome gained a nearly inexhaustible source of goods and manpower. Hadrian's own family had been transplanted from Spain to Italy where they had prospered, and even foreign divinities were incorporated by the Romans, beginning with the entire Greek pantheon.

The Carthaginians, seeing Romans as potential bullies, honored them early on. Already, in 351 BC, they gave Rome the gift of a huge crown of pure gold weighing 11 kilos, a gift so prized by the Romans that they put it in their most sacred temple, Jupiter Optimus Maximus on the Capitoline Hill. Romans and Carthaginians were then so close that they considered themselves citizens of each other's country.

But Roman power took a jump ahead as the Romans extended their influence over both northern and southern Italy, the south known as Magna Graecia, an area inhabited by Greek colonists. Rome destroyed the power of its leader, Pyrrhus, during a series of battles that Pyrrhus usually won, but at such severe cost to him that the total of his wins culminated in a huge loss of men and material. Pyrrhus was eventually forced return to Greece where, during a battle, an old woman knocked him unconscious by throwing a tile from a rooftop, allowing his capture and beheading. Thanks to Roman victories, other nations began to fear Rome, among them Egypt where the Greek ruler Ptolemy initiated diplomatic relations between the two countries.

Aroused by the immense financial gain and the equally immense military glory that came through conquest, Rome was quick to answer an appeal from Sicily for help fighting mercenaries expatriated from Magna Graecia when Pyrrhus sailed back to Greece. An appeal had also been sent to Carthage who coveted Sicily, hoping it would become the center of their trading empire. Carthage answered by sending a fleet to the island. At the same time, they attempted to keep the Romans from leaving the Italian port of Rhegium and landing on Sicily, the Carthaginian general Hanno promising that Carthaginian ships would prevent the Romans from even washing their hands in the sea. Rome nonetheless gained control over the eastern segment of Sicily, leaving the western part to Carthage, and Hanno was crucified for not keeping his word.

The Romans, comfortable only during land battles, had a fleet, but nothing in comparison to the Carthaginians'. They therefore set in motion a massive building campaign under the leadership of the consul Duilius. The ships were unwieldy but possessed crows, a Roman invention, long and narrow bridges equipped with spikes that were held in an upward position on the prows of the Roman ships until released when an enemy ship was close enough. The pointed spike was then driven into the enemy deck and held fast by the weight of the bridge, over which the Roman soldiers stormed, as they would during a battle on land. During an initial encounter with the Carthaginians, off the coast of Sicily, the Carthaginian sailors literally snickered at the sight of their Roman counterpart, so certain were they of victory over a fleet of tyros. They lost and their commander was crucified, while Duilius went on to Rome where he was honored with Rome's highest honor, a Triumph. The Romans, emboldened, then sailed on to pester Sardinia and Corsica.

The Carthaginians, unlike the Romans, depended heavily on mercenaries. They now sent to Sparta for Spartan general Xanthippus to help them in Sicily. At the same time, the Romans, emboldened by their naval successes, decided to invade North Africa, only the second time they had ever left Italy, the first being the invasion of Sicily. They were victorious until a storm sank nearly 300 of their ships, with the loss of 100,000 men. The Carthaginians too had victories in Sicily until, during one attack on Sicilian soil, the Romans took special care to wound the Carthaginian elephants. The animals, made mad with fear at seeing and hearing their fellow elephants cry out in pain, abruptly turned to retreat, trampling the Carthaginians and their mercenaries underfoot. Thirty thousand were thought to have died. The Roman commander, Metelus, later went to Rome for his Triumph, parading, through the narrow streets of the city, the elephants he had captured. Back in Sicily his Carthaginian counterpart was put to death, replaced by Hamilcar Barca who was not so much expected to take back the island from the Romans as to save what he could. When he failed, Carthage sued for peace. The terms were terrible: Sicily would be evacuated, all Roman prisoners freed, and an indemnity of 3,200 talents was to be paid, 1,000 immediately, the rest over a period of 10 years. In this way the First Punic War came to an end. (Punic, a Latin word, refers to peoples of Phoenician descent.)

After the war a great period of instability ensued. Mercenaries returning to Carthage revolted when not paid. The Carthaginians had attempted to control the mercenaries by recruiting them from different nationalities so that they literally couldn't speak the same language. The mercenaries were also dispersed throughout North Africa in small groups to keep them from uniting their forces, and their women and children were often taken hostage. The mercenaries nonetheless revolted. Battles of incredible cruelty followed wherein captives on both sides were tortured, their hands cut off and their legs broken, they were suffocated with their own genitals or buried alive, while others were nailed to crosses. Rome took advantage of the chaos by taking definitive control of Sardinia and Corsica. Hamilcar Barca chose that moment to lead his men to Spain. The Carthaginian fleet was in such poor repair that Hamilcar was forced to march on foot to the Pillars of Hercules where they crossed over to Hadrian's homeland. Hamilcar founded New Carthage, perfectly positioned for fishing and trade, and an excellent port for the expedition of silver that Carthaginian slaves extracted from Spanish mines. Hamilcar turned the reins over to his son, Hannibal, a man described by the historian Livy as reckless in courting danger, indefatigable, sleeping on the ground wrapped in his cloak, always first to attack and last to leave the battlefield.

Hannibal expanded the size of his Spanish empire until he controlled half of the peninsula. His mines produced 135 kilos of silver a day, making New Carthage rich. With an infantry of 60,000 and a cavalry of 8,000, he didn't hesitate to attack neighboring Saguntum, a town that immediately appealed to Rome for help. As Rome took its time in deciding the fate of the city, many of the inhabitants committed mass suicide, others surrendered. Hannibal shared the town's spoils with his soldiers and set aside the town's gold and silver for future use. In response Rome sent an embassy to Carthage demanding the return of Saguntum. When Carthage refused, Rome declared war.

While Hannibal made plans to invade Italy, a dangerous scheme because he would have to pass through the lands of hostile tribes as well as traverse the Pyrenees and the Alps, Roman Scipio decided to lead 22,000 men in an invasion of Spain by sea, at the same time that Roman general Tiberius Longus led a fleet of 160 ships in an attack on Carthage. The tables had now been turned, as Rome, a former land power, reigned supreme over the seas, obliging Carthage and Hannibal to rely on a land army. Hannibal's forces consisted of 12,000 men, many of them mercenaries. Carthage requested help from the south of Italy, from Magna Craecia. Greece and Carthage had a long history of friendship and trade, and Hannibal had been taught Greek history and literature by Greek tutors hired by Hannibal's father Hamilcar. In addition, it was the Greek Alexander the Great who had first used elephants in battle, 480 of them in his campaign in Syria. The Romans considered elephants as being untrustworthy, and indeed, when panicked they often turned on their own troops in an attempt to escape injury. This obliged their drivers to equip themselves with mallets carved to a sharp point that they drove into the elephant's spinal cord when the animal rebelled. Hannibal also engaged Celts from Gaul and the Po Valley, savages he considered appropriate cannon fodder.

But they knew how to fight. During a first battle against Scipio, Hannibal had the advantage of numbers and cavalry, and in addition, say the historical sources, sunlight and wind-blown dust blinded and choked the Romans. But Scipio escaped with his life, saved by his 17-year-old son. Longus was forced to give up his attack on Carthage and return to Italy. There, men captured by the Carthaginians were treated very differently. To force a wedge between Romans who had Roman citizenship and Italians outside of the city who didn't, Romans were imprisoned and starved, while native Italians were sent home with messages of peace.

To put an end to Hannibal, Rome nominated two new generals and supplied them with 87,000 troops, compared to Hannibal's 50,000. The two armies came together at the town of Cannae. Confronted by the better-trained and more experienced Carthaginians and their mercenaries, as well as the far superior Celtic horsemen, 70,000 Roman soldiers were killed and another 10,000 captured. On the battlefield the Roman wounded, mad with thirst and suffering from severe wounds, bared their necks to the blade of the enemy, begging for release. Livy tells us that some went so far as to bury their heads in the soil in an attempt to suffocate themselves. One Carthaginian mercenary was pulled from under a Roman soldier, his ears and nose torn off: the Roman, having lost his weapons, had bitten at his enemy with his teeth.

Thanks to his victory, Hannibal knew the time was right to send his brother Mago to Carthage for reinforcements. Mago shocked the Carthaginian Council by emptying the contents of a huge sack, the gold rings taken from the thousands of dead

Romans slaughtered at Cannae. Hannibal's request for more troops was granted, and Hannibal, after seven years of fighting in Italy, rode to the very gates of Rome. The alarm was such that the Romans resurrected a ritual extinct for a hundred years: they sacrificed two men and two women to the gods, Gauls and Greeks, all four buried alive.

Back in Spain, Scipio spread the word that he was the son of Zeus, Zeus who had impregnated Scipio's mother in the form of a snake, the form he preferred when not taking that of the head and neck of a swan. Scipio attacked and conquered New Carthage. He made friends of the New Carthaginians by freeing the population, and great wealth for Rome by seizing their silver mines. Hannibal's second brother, Hasdrubal, who had failed to save New Carthage, took his remaining troops to Italy to join Hannibal. His other brother Mago was killed on the way, as was Hasdrubal whose head, in a gesture of infamous cruelty, was decapitated and thrown into Hannibal's lines, the way in which Hannibal learned of his brother's slaying. Another piece of bad news came his way: Scipio had been sent to destroy Carthage.

Scipio started off by launching a surprise attack on a camp outside the city during the night, setting its wood and reed dwellings on fire. Sixty-three thousand men perished, forcing Carthage to immediately sue for peace. The terms were draconian: all prisoners would be released and Italian deserters put to death, all Carthaginian armies would be withdrawn from Spain, Italy and Gaul, all islands between Italy and Africa would be abandoned, the entire Carthaginian navy would be handed over, except for ten ships, and an indemnity of 10,000 talents would be paid to cover the war damage--but Carthage itself would not be razed. The ships were burned in the waters in front of Carthage and mercenaries, their former allies, had their throats cut in full view of Carthaginians. The Second Punic War came to an end and Scipio rose to near godhood, known for all time as Scipio Africanus.

Hannibal, after an amazing span of 15 years in Italy, fled to Asia Minor where he helped one prince after another in their wars against Rome. Finally cornered in Bithynia, homeland of Antinous, he took his life with poison.

Although Romans considered themselves pious and courageous, they were especially jealous of any other power around what they called "our sea". The historian Cato, who had taken part in the First Punic War, hated the Carthaginians so ferociously that he used every occasion to condemn them as future predators. The Senate therefore chose him to sail to Carthage to see if the population was as downtrodden as Carthaginian emissaries claimed they were. Cato discovered a city spilling over with wealth, whose citizens were vigorous and whose fighting men strong and outstandingly armed. He returned to Rome to warn of the danger, ending each of his speeches with the chilling words, Carthage must be destroyed!

The casus belli for Roman intervention was an attack by neighboring tribes on a stretch of fertile farmland owned by Carthage. The tribes begged for Rome to intervene, which it did by sending an embassy that, after viewing the situation, voted in favor of the tribes. Not only would Carthage be forced to render the land, but the city would also have to turn over all its arms, enough to equip an estimated 20,000 men. Carthage complied. Unarmed, Rome revealed the secret second part of its plan: Carthaginians could live under their own laws, but not under the skies over Carthage. The city had to be obliterated, along with its harbors and ships. The Romans pushed their bad faith so far as to assure the Carthaginians that as an exclusively agricultural nation they would be better off, since it was their ships and commerce which had been the cause of their troubles up to then.

The Carthaginians begged for a month's grace, during which they could send their own embassy to Rome to plead their cause. After the embassy had set off, they murdered every Italian within their walls, and during the thirty-day truce the Romans had granted them, the Carthaginians produced weapons. Each available space was turned into a workshop dedicated to producing swords, shields, spears and other arms. Even ships were built from whatever scrap could be unearthed.

Faced with a city again powerful, the Romans answered by sending a teenager to head their armies, a boy called Scipio

Aemilianus, Scipio Africanus' son--a boy, perhaps, but one with the Scipio name and, hopefully, the Scipio touch.

The description of the final battle for Carthage would take pages. The battle followed the usual form of others in the ancient world: naval blockades, the construction of a mole, breaching towers; Roman and Carthaginian captives inhumanly butchered in sight of their fellow citizens; and the final entry during which the Romans went from street to street, door to door, raping, maiming, killing and burning. Perhaps 50,000 Carthaginians were taken prisoner and sold into slavery. Carthage's chosen leader, Hasdrubal, and other dignitaries, were spared. One historian claims that Hasdrubal's wife cut the throats of his two sons in plain view of her traitor husband before leaping into the fire that eventually razed the city to the ground.

Romans murdered and pillaged, taking as loot women, stripping children naked and lashing them to carts like beasts of burden, forcing them under whip to return to the beaches with loads of loot. The children who collapsed on the trails to the ships were left to die, while others went mad. Yet a few made it to the surrounding woods where the Romans feared to pursue.

The runaways would return to the smoldering remains of their citadel on the days to follow, once the enemy had taken to the seas. The were too late to save their dead relatives from the horror of being mutilated by birds and animals, their bodies torn to pieces and devoured, their final resting place the belly of the beast. These would never know purification by incorruptible fire, nor would they have a burial mound where they would be honored by family and loved ones and passers-by. These would vanish from human memory, the most horrifying damnation known to Romans and Carthaginians alike.

For the survivors worse still was to come in the form of plague. This was neither instant death nor resurrection thanks to the funeral pyre. This came with a burning of the head and a bleeding of the throat, with pain in the chest and retching of the stomach, with pustules and ulcers and stinking flesh, with voiding bowels and feverish insanity. These even vultures did not venture to eat. The devout who raised pyres in accordance with eternal laws saw them stolen by those who got to them first with their own dead, or saw bodies thrown on the pyres where other cadavers were already in flame.

Lawlessness broke out, the strong plundered the weak, and with loss of heart came loss of belief in the mercy of the gods. Licentious acts of bestiality robbed Carthaginians of the last strands of unity that had held them together as a people. In straggly groups they wandered off, abandoning the city to the dust of ages.

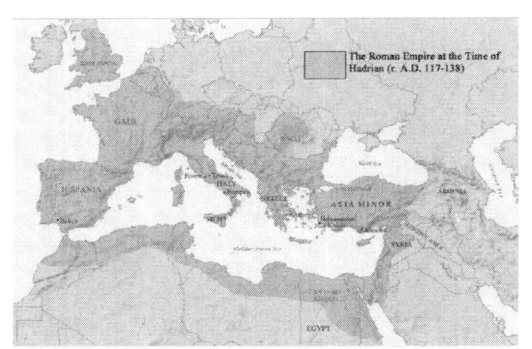

Hadrian's Empire.
The Romans subsisted by feeding on the outer world like a virus, which led Tacitus to write: ''The Romans make a desert and call it peace.

CHAPTER FOUR

≈ Hadrian Emperor ≈ Proscription ≈ Mithridates ≈

Before returning to Rome Hadrian made a series of decisions that had perhaps been in his mind for years. He couldn't rid himself of the 1,000-strong Praetorian Guard who meddled in the affairs of emperors, at times even choosing them, so he added to them by organizing his own Batavian Guard, imperial horsemen, made up of ferocious and totally trustworthy Germans. Knowing that he ruled thanks to his men, he immediately awarded them all a bonus. He as well kept up his and Trajan's custom of eating in their mess, marching alongside them and living in a tent as they did. He kept them disciplined through continual training, exercise and instruction in battle tactics. He loved the casualness and familiarity of camp life, the simplicity of his soldiers, the innocent laughter of young men over nothing, youths capable, nonetheless, of disemboweling the enemy and stuffing his privates into his dead or dying mouth, fresh complexioned youths as guileless naked as dressed.

Surprisingly, he did something very uncharacteristic for a Roman: he gave up land. Understanding that the countries far from home were costing Romans a fortune to maintain, he simply abandoned them. Parthia, Armenia, Mesopotamia and Assyria were put on the block, as well as parts of newly-conquered Dacia. Bridges across the Danube were felled as the easiest way of halting enemy incursions. He perhaps knew that Augustus himself had stated, after the shattering loss of three legions in the Teutoburg Forest massacre, that "Empire had to be kept within bounds". On the other hand, vital countries such as Egypt were given tax incentives in order to calm the population and assure foodstuffs for Italy.

He initiated reforms, the first of which dazzled Rome: He cancelled all unpaid debts that individuals owed the government, a sum thought to be around one billion sesterces. The debt forms were publically burned and a coin minted that showed the debts going up in smoke. Until then local authorities were forced to pay for the government's courier system--hotels, horses, carriages and the upkeep of the roads themselves--over which rode mail and officials. From then on the government would pay. Senators who could prove they were poor were given an allowance, as were needy government officials (which nonetheless didn't compensate, in senatorial eyes, for the four members he ordered murdered because they opposed his becoming emperor). But the strangest new law did not eradicate Proscriptions, it just turned over the monies gained from the property of condemned persons to the state, and no longer to the emperor in person.

Proscriptions are difficult for the modern man to wrap his mind around, so I would like to pause a moment to discuss the phenomenon. They began with Sulla but became rampant devises of murder and pillage during the Second Triumvirate (the First Triumvirate had been organized by Pompey the Great, Caesar and Crassus for the purpose of uniting their forces in order to win elections and influence people). The Second Triumvirate was between Marc Antony, Augustus (then called Octavian) and Lucius Lepidus. The purpose was to raise money to support the 43 legions necessary to hunt down and destroy Caesar's murderers, Brutus and Cassius (who were later joined by Pompey the Great). Because Antony and Augustus didn't trust each other, they met on an island, the riverbanks of which had 5,000 of Antony's soldiers on one side, 5,000 of Augustus' on the other. For two days, from dawn to dusk, they decided whom they would kill, either to loot their wealth or because they simply didn't like them. Lepidus sacrificed a brother, Augustus liquidated a former guardian. No relative or friend was spared. Over 300 senators were slaughtered. Even the imminently famous Cicero, whom Antony hated, had his head chopped off (caught fleeing in his carriage, he stuck out his scrawny neck and pleaded for his executioner to do the job properly). Informers who denounced a man--any man could be denounced by wives and children in need of lucre, by creditors, former slaves, and neighbors who wanted a man's land--were rewarded. Those who did the actual killing were given a part of the spoils. Even boys whose only guilt was having inherited money could find themselves on the list; they were immediately abandoned by their families and tracked like animals. Some men sought shelter down wells, in sewers, under rafters. The heads of victims were expedited to Antony who inspected them, at times, said one historian, over dinner. Augustus collected furniture, *objets d'art*, wonderful vases and priceless jewelry in this way. The Republic had truly come to an end, and a glorious exercise in democracy was buried for hundreds of years to come. The sad point is that Roman republicanism as well as Greek democracy had been, all along, based on slavery, which freed the people from hunting for food, building their lodgings, caring for their children, and multiple other burdens that would have kept Roman citizens from loafing in the Forum (or, in Athens, in the Agora). Just as Communism--a step forward for humanity--had been destroyed by murderous tyrants, so the likes of Augustus and Antony would eventually plunge Italy into the Dark Ages.

Caesar destroyed democracy and Augustus made the destruction palatable because he ruled with such loving great care, devoting all his time to his country and his family, destroying whatever harmed either, just as he destroyed his grandson Postumus: The lad had been sent to the island of Planasia, near Elba, because he had become totally uncontrollable. According to some sources he was one of those boys who would gleefully torture animals before setting his sights on his fellow man. Augustus wanted to make certain that he was beyond redemption before naming Tiberius, his wife Livia's son, his heir. The boy allowed the emperor to pamper him, he listened to the emperor's sweat talk, but Augustus, who knew boys well from having raised and studied them, knew the lad was beyond his reach. He held him close, one last time, promising that his imprisonment would soon be ended and they would be reunited, a pledge he kept by ordering the boy's guard to run him through with his sword, a long, wide, thick and very heavy instrument of murder. Augustus then returned to Rome where some believe he knew his wife was poisoning the figs he cultivated in his garden, a form of suicide because he felt that he had already lived too long. Weak, ugly and no longer able to contend with the deceit that encircled him, he wished to put an end to an incredibly full life. He indeed joined Postumus in a better place. Augustus' death only made things worse for Rome, for the emperors that came after him were like pustules on the cheeks of the ass: Tiberius smothered by Caligula, Caligula run through by his soldiers and Nero who committed suicide.

Suicide was an acceptable "out" among Romans. When trapped in impossible situations soldiers sought this honorable exit, the alternative being years of dishonorable imprisonment. One could also commit suicide for reasons of decency, as the best way to leave with dignity, thusly escaping the humiliation of degrading illness or the loss of one's reputation due to a scandal. It was a way to cease being a burden on one's family. The philosophers knew that suicide was merely the advancement of the inevitable and, as the Stoics maintained, only the relinquishing of something we have all just temporarily borrowed.

Because Hadrian knew the truth of the adage that Romans needed bread and circuses, he provided a supplement of grain and, to mark his 43rd birthday, gladiatorial games that lasted six days. Wooden balls there thrown into the bleachers with the names of various prizes such as objects of silver or gold, horses, livestock and even slaves. He was polite to everyone and understood that the people didn't like their ruler to read or write during the games, so he did as Augustus had done, he gave his full attention to what was going on in the arena. But he did seat men and women separately in the Circus Maximus racetrack and had them bathe separately in the baths. And also as Augustus had done, he made certain that cereals from Egypt and olive oil from Sicily were never lacking, and that the price of such goods was carefully controlled. Most importantly, he knew that what he decided had the weight of law, because the people had made him their emperor--a lesson learned from both Augustus and Trajan.

The Circus Maximus was a chariot racetrack, although occasionally used for other forms of mass entertainment, that seated 250,000 spectators. It was frequented by Hadrian who loved the races.

It was Juvenal who wrote that Hadrian provided the people with "bread and circuses", to which he could have added baths. Although Rome stank due to its dirty citizens, poor plumbing and defecating animals, and was noisy, the baths offered a moment of relaxation, even if no less noisy: overlapping conversations, hooting and laughter, venders hawking food and drink, and the occasional applause when someone supremely endowed strode by.

Hustlers displayed their wares and young boys didn't hesitate to show off their erections among themselves, proud they would soon be like the men in their midst. The baths were such a source of pleasure that woman complained to Hadrian that their husbands were no longer home enough and willing enough to do their marital duties. The *Historia Augusta* stated that Hadrian had a private word with some and, like Augustus, tried to get them to furnish the Empire with sons.

Hadrian chose the great Suetonius, the author of *On Famous Men* and his masterpiece *The Lives of the Caesars*, to be his personal secretary. Hadrian governed with an eye on everything. He surrounded himself with knights skilled in law, and worked through councils and committees, seeking help from everyone in the know, many of whom were senators. He had an open and original mind, and a taste for what was foreign. He liked the company of architects, engineers and artists, and was never out of the company of philosophers, rhetoricians and literati, lavishing pensions on them all. But he could be both touchy and jealous. When the architect Apollodorus criticized Hadrian's architectural creations, he had him put to death. Apollodorus had been Trajan's architect and had been responsible for Trajan's column, the Forum, baths and markets, constructions fueled by the spoils from the Dacian Wars. Hadrian's masterpiece was his Pantheon, in honor of the gods. Its magnificent dome contains 140 coffers of breathtaking beauty, as is the dome, crowned by an eye nine meters wide that admits light, rain and an occasional snowfall. The dome is made of concrete, a substance discovered during the 3rd century BC, a mixture of lime, water and substances like sand, and the Pantheon is the largest un-reinforced dome in the world (illustrated in the chapter on the Tibur complex). At times Hadrian held court and public audiences in the Pantheon, and it served as Rome's tribunal. It was Hadrian's love of domes that led to Apollodorus' murder, when the architect told Hadrian to ''go away and draw your pumpkins'' (a murder for which there is no historical evidence).

He preferred the Stoics but gave himself up to no specific philosophy or religion, nor did he deny any of them. He wrote poetry and was considered as much an artist as Nero, but without Nero's madness. Suetonius accompanied him on his many displacements, displacements Hadrian deemed necessary because a ruler could only know what was really going on in the empire by going into the provinces himself. Thus began years of wandering.

He went through Gaul to Britannia where his famous wall was already under construction. As the area it spanned was nearly empty of human life, the reason for his decision to build it is questioned. Perhaps he simply wished to separated Romans from the barbarians to the north, or he might have wished to control immigration or prevent smuggling. From Britain he went through Spain to Mauretania in the north of Africa, then east to Libya and on to the Euphrates and the Black Sea, Anatolia and Pontus.

80 miles (129 kilometers) long, 10 feet thick, 14 feet high, it was fronted by a ditch 20 feet deep.

The wild lands of Pontus that Hadrian traversed had been ruled by one of the most ruthless murderers in human history, Mithridates, whose birth had been announced by a comet, the brightness of which obscured even the sun. Mithridates' father had built up a huge army of locals from Cappadocia, Phrygia, Pontus and Greece, and soon controlled the entire southern shore of the Black Sea. When his father was assassinated by his wife who ruled as regent in favor of her younger son, Mithridates was forced to flee the capital, Amaseia. While his mother made friends with the Romans, Mithridates reinforced the ranks of the men who had fled with him with mercenaries from Crete and Gaul, and Galatians from the highland of Anatolia who fought stark naked, a protection against being infected by filthy clothing when wounded. Returning to Amaseia, he had his mother and younger brother thrown into a dungeon and left to starve. He married his sister and founded his own dynasty. A superb horseman and archer, he exercised daily, endowing himself with an anatomy he so admired that he had armor shaped to captured the exact contours of his abs and pectorals, a copy of which he sent to Delphi to be admired by the god Apollo--an expert in boys' abs and pectorals, among other anatomical points of interest (3).

Mithridates

Since Rome was an ever-invasive power, and as Roman legions were as hopeless on water as they were valiant on land, Mithridates decided to build a navy. The navy became an obsession, as did his belief that, like his father, he would be poisoned. He prepared himself for the eventuality by taking small daily doses of poison. The precaution saved his life when his sister-wife tried to kill him in order to place their eight-year-old son on the throne. In her way she had been as effective as Hadian had been in his: both used sex, she to turn Mithridates' supporters by sleeping with one and all, Hadrian by winning over Trajan's followers through his promiscuous inseminating of Trajan's advisors. She too was immured. When the Romans saw that Mithridates was gaining increasing power by bringing Bithynia, the homeland of Antinous, to his side, and by overpowering the Scythians, an act of war that even Cyrus the Great and Alexander the Great had failed to accomplish, the Romans sent troops to douse his ardors. While they were on their way, Mithridates used the time to bring Cappadocia over to his side. He did so by requesting a meeting with the king of Cappadocia. As Mithridates was feared, the king had him intimately searched before being allowed access. Mithridates is said to have stopped the searcher from going too far by noting, when the man placed a hand on his groin, that he didn't share the man's pederastic tastes. Once inside the room he withdrew a knife lodged between his legs and bled the king like the pig he was. He then made certain that his allies would be fully bound to him by committing an act that the Romans would never forgive. He sent secret messages to every corner of Asia Minor, ordering the peoples to slaughter all Romans in their midst, 80,000 men, women and children. Such was the hatred for Italians that in some places parents were obliged to witness the murder of their children, then men the slitting of their wives' throats before their own deaths, most often by suffocating on their own genitals (during the times of Marco Polo, the Great Kahn got the same result by stuffing the mouths of his enemies with shit, while in Afghanistan men were pegged out on their backs, their mouths forced open with sticks, over which women squatted and peed, drowning them). Roman slaves were freed and half of all the debts the peoples had owed the Romans were forgiven, the other half went to Mithridates. He dealt with the rulers of provinces that he was unsure of in a way adopted by the Mafia thousands of years later. They were invited to a banquet during which the doors were locked, permitting Mithridates' men to kill them all.

Rome sent legions to deal with the king once and for all. Most of the commanders, avenging the death of the 80,000, showed no mercy as they went from one of Mithridates' client countries to another, raping, massacring and stealing anything of value, burning everything that wasn't. One young commander earned the sobriquet *"carnifex adulescens"*, "teenage butcher". Some commanders spared towns if they gave up immediately, knowing that it was the best way to save the lives of their troops. As many leaders had been murdered in the Mafia-style dinners, the towns were more than happy to go over to Rome. One noted holdout surprised the Romans by releasing bears and wasps on them as the Romans attempted to tunnel under the fortifications.

His back up against the wall, Mithridates ordered his harem to commit suicide by taking poison. One member, the mother of one of his sons, chose to have her throat cut by a eunuch while wearing the royal diadem. (Eunuchs were capable of having erections despite the loss of their testicles, so they were often obliged to have the penis severed at the root.) Mithridates too took poison, but due to years of building up resistance, he was forced to ask his servant to give him eternal release by the sword.

From Pontus Hadrian went on to Bithynia where he met the boy of his life.

BOOK TWO

CHAPTER FIVE

≈ Roman Virility and Greek Love of Boys ≈
≈ Part 1 ≈

All historical sources conclude that the Romans couldn't care less if a man stuck his dick in a girl or a boy: it just didn't matter. Caesar himself was known to be a man to every woman, a woman to every man. His soldiers sang ditties to that effect as they marched along, to Caesar's feigned amusement; in fact, Caesar was far more sensitive about losing his hair than having lost his cherry, when young, to King Nicomedes who happened to have been a Bithynian like Antinous, and like Antinous Nicomedes was noted for the dimensions of his member. The words hetero and homo didn't exist yet because the distinction between them was immaterial.

Whereas Greek boys were encouraged to have older lovers and to learn from them, the Romans had sex for pleasure as long as the participants respected two iron-clad principles (although, as we all well know, all iron-clad principles are made to be disregarded): A Roman male could not have sex with another Roman male. If he was horny and a slave (or a foreigner or anyone else, as long as he wasn't a Roman) passed by, he or she was fair game. The second principle was that a Roman male had to do the penetrating. It was he who was virile (*vir* meaning manly in Latin). A corollary to the two principles was the very strong preference for young smooth hairless bodies, often between the ages of 14 and 20, marked by the onset of down on the boy's cheeks (permissible too on his butt cheeks). Greek boys had Greek lovers, often many, from whom the boys gained the key to life: *knowledge*. The boys were normally passive, the men active, and when the boys became men, the roles were inversed: they took on a boy of their own, their belovèd, and they became the boy's lover and teacher. There was also a practical side to Greek love. A lover would never ever show weakness before his belovèd and vice versa, which made them the fiercest fighting force the world has ever known, the steel that forged the 300 of Leonidas (3) and the Sacred Band (9).

The Romans and Greeks practiced vaginal and anal penetration, intercrural insertion, fellatio and cunnilingus. Mutual masturbation and circle jerks were rarely mentioned because they were so common between schoolboys, a little like boys pissing together, and perhaps also because this took place between Roman boys. Parents despaired of keeping their sons, if they were beautiful, chaste. Roman boys did have access to slaves, just like their elders did, on whom they could practice intercourse, intercrural or anal. As today, the Romans associated homosexual relations with Greece (in France one says, for the English Go Fuck Yourself: *Va te faire voir chez les Grecs*). Diogenes the Cynic (see Sources) stated that of the three appetites, food, drink and sex, sex was the easiest to fulfill as one need only rub oneself to obtain instant satisfaction.

Sex was found in brothels and latrines and taverns, parks and gardens and any other place sheltered from public view. Hadrian's successor, Lucius Verus, opened a tavern in his own home in order to create a climate for debauch, and Elagabalus stationed himself outside his place, taking on all comers, a male Messalina.

Prostitutes showed their wares in parks and gardens as they do today, and many turned to acting to supplement their incomes, as did Hadrian's favorite, the mime Pylades. As just being a wife was enough status for most women, men were free to look elsewhere for pleasure. In Rome love was always in the air (just like today). The Romans had adopted many of the Greek gods and their myths, especially those which dealt with Apollo and Hyacinth, Hercules and Hylas, Achilles and Patroclus, Zeus and his cupbearer and bedmate Ganymede. Once in the Louvre, in the Salle des Vases Grecques, while I was admiring a vase showing the bearded Zeus looking over his shoulder at Ganymede, a boy entered. It was Philippe, who became my very first lover, the story of which is in my autobiography (1). Antinous' role was strikingly similar to that played by Ganymede, and as he was Greek he was a safe foreigner, although it's doubtful that Hadrian would have turned him away should he have been a Roman citizen. The Greeks were not obliged to look for sex in gardens or taverns or back alleys. They had gymnasiums where they could openly entice boys, although men were not allowed to frequent boys there who were under age 18. Rich parents sent slaves to accompany their sons to and from the gym. Male-male sex was nonetheless so current that we have the story of the Greek boy who didn't share his schoolmates' interest in men. He prayed to Zeus so that he too could be moved by the love of boys, but when this failed to happen, he committed suicide.

A huge difference between the Greeks and the Romans (if historians, after two thousand years, are correct; let us not forget that there isn't one word in Homer concerning homosexual relationships) was that the Greeks preferred their boys with modest members, whereas the Romans followed the cult of Priapus, and, as today, thought that bigger was always better. Clapping could be heard in the Roman baths when a man of healthy dimensions paraded through the corridors, and one Roman, Cotta, was known to invite only guests to his lavish dinners whom he had first seen at the baths--a word often on his lips was donkey. Presumably, even heteros today show deferential admiration for those who show more manliness than they do themselves, which does not necessarily mean they sexually desired them. Roman boys often wore phallic amulets to protect them from the evil eye, and even today Roman men and boys quickly touch their balls to ward off evil, as when, for example, they see a passing priest.

Some hoopla developed concerning the roles of the lover and his belovèd. Lovers didn't just fall in love with any boy, but only those who showed intelligence and maturity. But if this were true, wondered Cicero, why do lovers only fall in love with handsome youths and never ugly ones? The sexual link was ephemeral and came to an end with the growing of a first beard. From then on the boy and lover became loyal friends and remained so throughout their lives.

Boys, then as now, were mantraps: The poet Tibullus tells us that we have no chance against tender youths, who give us ample reason to love them. This boy is pleasing due to the masterly control he has over his horse; this other one causes our hearts to flutter when he breaks the surface of the water, showing his snow-white chest and nipples; so and so captures us by his daring; such and such by his peaches-and-cream complexion. At times youths objected for the form when men made advances, even menacing to tell their fathers if the men didn't cease. But once bridled, and the man could find rest after expulsing his lust, it was the boy who sought more, awaking the man from sleep by the gentle entreating of his buttocks. Again satisfied, man and boy plunged back into the arms of Morpheus for an hour before the boy asked if the man would like to do it again. The man would, but when the boy stirred still again, an hour later, it was the man who threatened the boy, "If you don't stop I'll tell your daddy!"

Boys also lacked fidelity, as in this letter sent from one Kurnos to his lover Timaleus, away at war. "Dear Timaleus, it is I, Kurnos. Many a friend has come and gone since you left, but it is to you that my thoughts return. Whenever I see Themis' horses, I think of my friend Timaleus. Remember how we stole rides before Eos' early light, and galloped across the fields like a single rider on his dapple mare--I've quite forgotten her name. She's grown too old to support one as sturdy as I, but she foaled just after you went away, and the little colt has long since borne my weight. Do you regret my sending you on campaign? I only stayed a month with Saurus and from then after missed only you. Come back home, my dear friend, and do not upbraid me harshly, for it is as the poet said: 'Boys and horses are the same. A horse does not cry for his rider thrown into the dust, but carries another man and eats his corn; a boy, too, only loves his current friend.' "

The role of a boy wasn't always easy either. Men liked them soft enough to caress, but not so soft as to be effeminate. Boys might relish being penetrated, but not enough to be mistaken for a woman. If the boy seemed too eager he could open himself to abuse, as men abused girls who were too available. Boys were often believed to be easily impaled because the anal muscles were supple, due to the fact that they hadn't as yet turned into real men. But rent-boys were often called upon to sodomize men who lusted for anal contact, as they had when young, because their anuses itched for what only an erect penis could scratch.

Fellatio and cunnilingus were both looked down upon as being unclean. The former, fellatio, was often associated with grown men with beards. Women were there for fucking, boys for sodomy and bearded men for cock sucking. Another degrading aspect was the use of sex to further one's advancement. From multiple sources we learn that this was Hadrian's way with Trajan's entourage: he advanced through fucking the emperor's influential friends, and by being fucked by them. But given the known promiscuous nature of Trajan's court, and the incredible sexual arousal in a climate of lustful males, most of whom were not simply Trajan's buddies but youths recruited to fulfill the needs of the emperor and his associates, Hadrian's task had certainly not been arduous.

Socrates warned about kissing Alcibiades' handsome son: "The beast they call young and handsome is more dangerous than a scorpion. You needn't touch a boy as you do a scorpion to be poisoned. A boy, with just a look, can make you mad from a distance. So when you see a beautiful boy run for your life, take a year's holiday elsewhere as it will take that long to heal you."

The Greek ideal of how fathers should raise their sons was, as usual, based on the gods. Zeus, for example, had excellent relations with his sons Hermes and Apollo. Here is a scene in which Zeus is explaining to Apollo just how smart Hermes is:

"I've never seen anyone so clever. A while back, for instance, Hermes and I were scrounging around Earth on some business or other--no, not what you're thinking, there were no petticoats involved--and being hungry and tired we stopped in at a peasant's hut along the way. Well, Son, you know how lowly and miserably those humans live. I had to destroy them once by sending that great flood, so sick had I become of seeing their despicable ways. We stopped at some peasant's hovel and to our astonishment we were hospitably offered warm wine and victuals. To thank the old man, Hermes and I asked him to confide his heart's innermost wish. The poor old fellow sighed and said that although he was impotent and his wife long dead, his heart's desire was to have a son.

"Now, I would have instructed him to eat a certain potent mushroom that has wondrous regenerative powers and then get himself a mistress. But not Hermes. After some thought he told the old man to go to his wife's grave and take out her bones. He was then to sacrifice a bull to Almighty Myself, skin the hide into which he would place his wife's bones, piss on the remains, and bury the hide and its contents in his wife's grave. At the end of nine months he was to return and dig it all up.

"The old man did as instructed, and when he returned nine months later he found a boy at the bottom of the pit, swaddled in the old hide. We named him 'Orion', which is Greek for 'He-Who-Makes-Water', a word that morphed into 'urine'." (5)

In the ancient world, as today, boys and men knew pining, tears, longing, despair, self-sacrifice--the entire panoply of sentiments. In Thebes the Sacred Band was formed, 300 lovers and their belovèds, fed at public expense and housed on the acropolis, they formed a group of warriors who would sacrifice themselves at the snap of a finger for their companions. Love between men was so special in Thebes that it was, says Plato, illegal for anyone to maintain that sex between men was *not* beautiful (9). Thanks to the Sacred Band Thebes freed itself from Spartan domination, until it was totally destroyed by Alexander the Great, he who was said to have known defeat only once in his life, when confronting the thighs of his lover Hephaestion (4).

Naturally, had there been only homosexuals in Thebes, Thebans would have died out. Plutarch relates the story of a rich Theban woman who arranged the kidnapping of a handsome ephebe that she then kept at her side until he understood that she was as interested in his welfare as she was her sexual satisfaction. She married the lad, to the fury of his male suitors. (This brings to mind the wonderful scene in *Some Like It Hot* in which Jack Lemmon returns from his date with Osgood and declares to Tony Curtis that they're going to get married. "But why would a guy marry another guy?" asked Curtis. "For *security*!" exclaims Lemmon.) There is also the story of Heracles' passage through Thebes where he slept, during a single night, with the forty-nine virgin daughters of the same father. The fiftieth daughter refused him and in anger he sentenced her to remain a virgin until the end of her life. Girls, however, got the best of Heracles when his boyfriend, the beautiful Hylas, abandoned him for nymphs that resided in a spring (which may have meant, in reality, that during their relationship Hylas drowned).

At any rate, a good father always had a ready tale for his son's ears. Zeus told Hermes about the Trojan War, but as the story was long and the boy appeared to be asleep ... well ... let the poet finish: "Almighty Zeus interrupted his story and looked down at this son. Hermes' arm and head rested unmoving on Zeus' leg. Zeus thought he had fallen asleep, and softly tried to disengage himself. But Hermes raised his head. There was the same look of intelligence and anticipation, although with anxiety least Almighty Father wish not to continue. Zeus hadn't the heart to abridge his promise to tell the story of the Great War. So after taking a few moments out while he put more tree trunks on the fire, stopped the moon and stars in their course and issued orders to Sleep--who owed him a favor--to make this night thrice, he returned to his throne, Hermes again at this knees, and while running his fingers through his son's auburn locks, Almighty Father picked up the thread of his tale without the loss of a single strand." (5)

CHAPTER SIX

≈ The Boy ≈

We don't know where and how they met, but most probably it was in Antinous' hometown, Claudiopolis, a citadel surrounded by mountains and known for its cows, milk and cheese. It was probably at a banquet of some kind, as emperors do not normally pick up boys off the streets. Perhaps it took place as it had when Mithridates met one of his wives, at an informal reception. The next morning the girl's father awoke to find that during the night someone had stuffed the cupboards of his home with gold and silverware, and added a white steed to his stable. But then, men among themselves have another regard on the subject. Far from being obliged to offer gold and silver they need only exchange a brief look before sharing their bodies.

The Boy

No one knows either what went on, physically, between the man and the boy, but we can hope that it took place often and lustily, that Hadrian showed tender affection and rough vigor when the moment demanded it, that they were clean in body and dirty in the way that only the human animal can be. I'm not going to invent the lascivious scene when, for the first time, they found themselves alone and randy (is there another word?)--with Internet even kids know what goes on between the sexes. But I do hope the experience included tears as well as laughter, because nothing in nature can be more exquisite and inspiring than love in general, love between youths in particular.

Antinous
111 – 130 AD

We're unaware, too, of the intensity of their love. Some historians write that the fascination of Marc Antony (and Caesar, for that matter) for Cleopatra was sincere and deeply sensual, other historians scoff at the idea, affirming that both Antony and Caesar were too experienced--and had, at their beck and call, too many other "candidates"--to fall head over heels for the Egyptian Ptolemy, and that the battle between Antony and Augustus had nothing at all to do with a mere woman. Some declare that Paris, Prince of Troy, was trapped into war over Helen, understanding his folly only when surrounded by Greeks (6); still others say the boy was obsessed and that Helen indeed had the beauty, charm and sexual appeal to launch a thousand ships. This was perhaps the case with the Bithynian youth.

The man

In my Introduction I mentioned visiting a restaurant overlooking the Parthenon with my lover, to whom I recounted the story of Hadrian and Antinous. I gave the short version, the one in which Antinous, grateful for the many favors Hadrian had accorded him, went to the oracle of Siwa and asked how he, a poor boy, could repay Hadrian's generosity. The oracle declared that if Antinous went to the Nile and drowned himself, all the years he would have lived would be added to those of Hadrian. The next day the boy's body was brought to the surface in a fish net. In remembrance of what they had shared, Hadrian raised a hundred cities that bore his belovèd's name and ordered the sculpting of a thousand statues. The boy's act of self-sacrifice brought tears to my lover's eyes and tears to my own, as it was I who had inspired this moment of emotion. He smiled through his tears and said, *À present, je sais ce qui me reste à faire!* (he was French, as am I)--"I now know what's expected of me!" (1)

Hadrian founded the city of Antinoupolis in Egypt, and had Antinous' beauty perpetuated in hundreds of statues, busts, sacred images, steles and coins. Here he's pictured as an Egyptian god.

A word about Siwa: It was propitious that Antinous chose that oracle because it was not only to Siwa that Alexander the Great had gone to ask the oracle for permission to deify his lover Hephaestion, but Siwa was a historical site for the assembly of homosexuals. In fact, it was there that, for the first time in the history of humanity, same-sex marriages were performed. Some historians think that the acceptance of male-male mating sprang up in Siwa in very ancient times in order to sanctify relationships between workers who, despite the extremely hostile topography and climate--too hostile for women--were there to work the land. The Egyptologist George Steindorff related that in 1900 marriages still took place between men and boys in Siwa with the boy being paid fifteen pounds, a huge sum for the time and the place. In 1917 an Arab historian, writing for the Harvard Museum, indicated that a man could have four wives but only one boy to whom he was bound by stringent obligations. Anthropologist Walter Cline claimed, in 1937, that all men and boys in Siwa practiced sodomy, and spoke as openly about it as they did about their relations with women. Prominent fathers would lend their sons to each other. Novelist Robin Maugham was told, in 1940, that women were mistreated but that men at Siwa would kill each other over a boy.

In his lost autobiography Hadrian related that Antinous had fallen into the Nile, and that he had seen Antinous' star rise from the waters into the heavens.

We don't know where or how they met, but most historians believe that soon afterwards the boy was sent to Rome to be education at the Paedogogum where he would learn the proper way to serve the emperor. There, the boys' ages varied from 12 to 18. They became secretaries, valets, accountants and pages, Trajan's weakness. They learned the three Rs and how to serve food and drink. As boys will be boys, and the school had dormitories, the Paedogogum was known for its vice. In the ruins that exist to this day graffiti has been found, one of which shows a boy on his knees in front of a cross that displayed a man whose head was in the form of an ass. Under it is scrawled, "Alexamenos worships this god", Alexamenos being, perhaps, a young Christian ribbed by fellow inmates.

Greek education in general, and certainly that of Antinous, began at home and centered, when not playing with toys as today, on learning right from wrong. At around age 7 boys attended elementary school or private schools where they were trained in gymnastics. Older boys ran, boxed, wrestled and threw the discus and javelin. Younger boys did calisthenics. As the boys were naked, girls were not allowed. (Girls were at home learning domestic work, except in Sparta where they received formal physical education and learned to run the city when the men were away.) The physical exercise trained the boys for later military service and it was good for both their health and their appearance. The three Rs and literature (meaning Homer) were the heart of their schooling. As books were rare and expensive, they did much reading aloud and much memorizing. They learned to dance and play the harp, flute or lyre.

Hadrian initiated the cult of Antinous, stating that he himself had seen Antinous' star rising from the Nile, proof of his resurrection. The Greek Antinous was allied with Roman Dionysus, himself the god of rebirth, and Osiris, reborn through the care of Isis, a new cult that was in direct competition with Christianity, both founded on resurrection and eternal life.

Around age 14 parents who could afford it sent their youngsters to philosopher-tutors. Poorer boys became apprentices at some trade. Under the philosopher-tutors they learned biology, chemistry, geometry, astronomy, music, arithmetic, oratory and rhetoric. The more the boys were educated, the more they were respected by their peers. The best and the brightest went on to be the Pericles and the Alcibiades of antiquity. They passed their free time, as did their elders, discussing politics and taking in plays at outdoor amphitheaters. The majority of the Greeks lived from farming and, thanks to their slaves, were free to pursue intellectual interests in the towns, or they could while away the time playing marbles, dice, checkers and knucklebones (today's jacks: a stone was thrown into the air and objects gathered up before it fell back). The main crops were grapes, olives, barley and wheat. Olive oil served for food and furnished light, as well as beauty products. Men applied it to their bodies before exercising and scraped it away afterwards with a strigil, leaving the skin clean.

Where Antinous was born the military played a more important role than in most other parts of Greece. Boys did their service in a kind of boot camp where they built up their strength and endurance, and trained to become as invincible as Spartans of old.

Antinous' cult spread throughout the Roman Empire, all of Greece, Egypt, North Africa and Spain, his bust even found in Britain at Littlecote Villa in Wiltshire.

Did they have sex before Antinous left Hadrian's side? It largely depends on the boy's age at the time of their meeting. He may have been 13 or 14, he may have been pubescent or he may not have been. Hadrian, as far as we know, was no pedophile. To be sexually attractive, the boy would have been hairless, naturally, other than the first signs of pubic and underarm down. Had Antinous been prepubescent he most probably left for Rome as virginal as when Hadrian first met him--although in things sexual nothing of a definitive nature can ever be advanced.

After a great deal of travel Hadrian returned to Rome where he found the Pantheon he had commissioned completed. At first built by Augustus' great and faithful friend Agrippa, it had burned to the ground. Now it had risen from its ashes, one of the few great monuments from the period that has come down to us. The inside is magnificent, and at the time of Hadrian the roof had been covered with gold leaf. Hadrian then withdrew to the enormous complex of buildings still under construction at Tibur.

CHAPTER SEVEN

≈ Tibur ≈

Hadrian's decision to build his official residence 21 miles from Rome was to ensure his privacy, with the added benefits of clean air and surrounding farms that supported him and his guests with fresh produce. What is called his villa was open to guests and bureaucrats who made the trips from the capital so he could conduct his business, and thanks to Roman roads and postal service, he was as well connected, given the times, as we are today.

Hadrian's villa (called the Villa Edriana in Italian), was located at Tibur (today's Tivoli). A villa was a Roman country house, in Hadrian's case an immense complex of buildings. Besides being a site of scenic beauty, Spanish expatriates had lived in the area for years, something that may have attracted him, along with Tibur having been favored by his wife Vibia Sabina, whose family is believed to have owned land in the region. Her visits may have been rare, as Hadrian's villa was a stag affair. One of the rare females in permanent occupation was the childhood wet-nurse he adored, Germana, who certainly made it a priority to turn a blind eye on the happenings around the pools and in the shaded bedrooms, although she would have forgiven him everything. She lived on, in luxury, until well after his death. Despite the already isolated nature of the villa, during Hadrian's residence his immense personal island was surrounded by walls, in addition to which a network of tunnels for the use of servants has been recently discovered (2013), a further guarantee that Hadrian's pool and quarters, and those of his guests, were beyond intrusion, voyeurism and any other form of prying.

Hadrian's dome-covered palace surrounded by a circular swimming moat.

The area where Hadrian could retreat for still more intimacy was a central island surrounded by a circular waterway or moat, itself surrounded by a portico with a roof supported by pillars, called a peristyle, offering a shaded walkway. As seen in these pictures, the 40 pillars of the portico were not fluted, while columns on the island were, proof of luxury.

Hadrian designed and named sections of the Tibur complex after the sites that had most impressed him in his travels, the Lyceum, the Academy, the Poikile and the Prytaneum, all in Athens; the Canopus, pictured above, found on the Nile delta; and the Vale of Tempe from Thessaly. He had works of art shipped in from all corners of the Empire, mostly Greek masterpieces. A unique hydraulic system was installed for his lakes, pools, waterways, fountains and canals, the whole contributing to a Paradise on earth.

Steps from the central island led into the water, a pool used for swimming and skinny dipping, a moat of protection more symbolic than real, certainly an additional warning that those who breached it would be severely dealt with.

The island was the center of a maze, and only Hadrian's most valued associates, friends and government officials had access when specifically invited, as did his most faithful servants. Those arriving at the Tiber complex entered a great reception vestibule, complete with baths where men could cleanse themselves and rooms where they could rest after the ride from Rome or the outer regions of the Empire. Food and drink were furnished, and there is no reason to not believe that the servants, of both sexes, were amiable to offering massages and otherwise lighten a visitor's stay, one source indicating that Hadrian employed, in one function or another, thousands of attendants. From the vestibule visitors were led to wherever the emperor wished to receive them, most likely on the outer limits of the maze or along the walkway giving onto the island, the inner sanctuary reserved for those he had met when under the guardianship of Trajan, others he had grown up with, childhood friends who had known him intimately and had been intimately known by him, boys become men he was free to be himself with.

Another view of the Canopus

The island's central construction was a domed edifice, a replica of the Roman Pantheon Hadrian had also constructed.

Hadrian's Pantheon in Rome. The similarly domed palace he constructed on his Tibur island could not have been less luxurious.

Island rooms were decorated with marine animals, tritons, mythological figures, mosaics and statuary, beds and couches of the finest fabrics, busts of Trajan and other men worthy of respect. There were private latrines, another luxury as using latrines was public, a social event where men met and talked, servants there with soft brushes at the end of long handles to wipe them clean. There were steam baths, a fountain and most likely a library.

The Tibur complex was serviced by perhaps thousands of people, all of whom were especially active during Hadrian's many absences, building, making repairs, cleaning the rooms, pool and gardening.

On the grounds of the complex was a serapeum, a site dedicated to the god that most historians believe Ptolemy I of Egypt invented in order to unite Greeks and Egyptians, while others state that the god already existed and was brought into favor by Ptolemy. The god was Greek in appearance with Egyptian trappings, and represented both abundance and resurrection. Serapis was of importance to Hadrian because he was derived from Osiris, dear to the emperor due to Osiris' resurrection, and during the Roman period Serapis replaced Osiris as the consort of Isis.

Serapis, an ancient Egyptian god revived by Ptolemy in order to unite Greeks and Egyptians, but given the head of a man because Romans had difficulty accepting animal-headed figures.

Tiber was originally a Etruscan site. The writer Athenaeus of Naucratis (see Sources) stated that the Etruscans were a people who held the most dissolute of bacchanalia. Both men and women took elaborate care of their bodies, shaven hairless, the men proud to show themselves naked, as did the woman, if not as often. Nights spent in drinking and lascivious discourse ended in intercourse where husbands shared their wives and took advantage of the wives of others, where youths and boys were especially sexually prized. The resultant children were brought up without the slightest care of who fathered them. Vice did not exist, just pleasure.

What took place on the island was anal intercourse. There may have been intercrural insertion (between the thighs), but one wonders why. Normally the boy was the target of intercourse, but Hadrian might have craved being penetrated, since for many men this is the most erotically satisfying form of sex. Both may have liked fellatio too, performing it and having it performed, as the male member is a consummate attraction for nearly all men, homosexual or not (7).

Hadrian was an intense hunter, a form of sport looked down upon by many aristocratic Romans, and was often reserved for slaves and freedmen. Hunting was, however, popular in Greece, which buttressed his Hellenism. Antinous too seems to have been an accomplished hunter, and both man and boy spent days in hunting pursuits. Often one has the misapprehension that because a boy allowed himself to be sodomized, he was somehow effeminate. Not so in ancient Greece and Rome. The Theban 300 consisted of men and their boys, all of the highest, most masculine, most valiant nature. This was true too of Leonidas and the band of lovers who nearly succeeded in destroying the armies of Xerxes before they were themselves cut down at Thermopylae--each of them certainly proud of filling his obligation to his lover and his beloved (3). Antinous was known to have been an accomplished athlete. Were he here today it would be among surfers or gymnasts or boxers that we would find him.

Of course, there were boys who frequented the coiffeurs and the oil shops and the perfume stoas, who highlighted their hair with gold, sculptured their pubic bushes, shaved their underarms and pre-oiled their buttocks, but men like Hadrian wanted real boys, the likes of Antinous.

CHAPTER EIGHT

≈ Roman Virility and Greek Love of Boys ≈
≈ Part 2 ≈

Augustus never ceased tongue-whipping the nobility because they weren't showing the example to the people by producing more progeny, which meant more farmers, more government servants and, especially, more soldiers. It must never be forgotten that for Rome incessant war was a source of wealth in various goods, land (especially land for soldiers upon their retirement), agricultural products and slaves--slaves that ran the economy thanks to their work and they were often the teachers and philosophers who gave direction to Roman life and culture (slavery, a fact of life, as it was in the United States until 1863).

Hadrian was absorbed by mysticism, the occult, fortune telling and the like, and spells that could not only bring one a lover or assure the death of an enemy, but could also help in one's sexual performance--supernatural aphrodisiacs. Pornography was an aid and walls were often covered with erotic frescos. Prostitution was legal, public and practiced everywhere. Males were naturally attracted to boys as well as girls, and although words for homosexual or heterosexual didn't exist in any form, there were numerous words for effeminacy. Again: virility comes from the Latin *vir*, but is also found in the word virtue, meaning that it was deemed appropriate to control one's sexual appetites.

There was, naturally, no *legal* age for sex in Greece. The boys involved were of military age, which infers that they had left boyhood. In Greece love between males was simply the socially accepted erotic friendship between a man and a boy, a boy between the ages of 15 to 17 (many Greeks referred to 16 as the perfect age for the belovèd, so perfect poets reserved it for the gods). In Crete it seems to have been a vital ingredient in military life, sanctioned by Zeus himself, an active lover of boys. Still, many scholars have found it strange that it was not commented on at all in Homer (a reason, perhaps, why Hadrian eventually turned away from Homer to the benefit of other writers such as Herodotus, Plato, Athenaeus and Xenophon, Xenophon whom Hadrian adored). In all other aspects of Greek life male-worship was clearly apparent: nude athletics, nude sculptures of ephebes (kouroi), historically famous cohorts of men and boys such as the Sacred Band of Thebes and the 300 of Themopylae, as well as-- with very few exceptions--the utter exclusion of women.

From this distance in time it's hard to pin down the behavior of the belovèd. Some poets claim that his role was passive in the sense that he contented himself with being beautiful, looking meekly at the ground as his lover greets him, allowing the man to stroke his cheek and gently nudge his genitals through the boy's chiton, the light tunic he wore that fell to the knees. Today this would seem erotic and daring, but also how arousing! Perhaps the lad did feel he had to play a submissive role, but I'm sure all masks fell away while he was being, later and in private, tenderly caressed by his lover.

A Greek chiton

In Crete a boy was abducted by a lover who, in concord with the boy's friends, takes the lad into the countryside where they spend two idyllic months hunting, feasting and exhausting their young bodies. The belovèd is then returned home with the symbolic gifts of military dress, an ox and a drinking cup (and whatever else the man might wish him to have, the expense of which would depend on the man's resources). Interestingly, the boy was then known by a Greek word meaning "he who stands ready," perhaps signifying Ganymede who, after being abducted by Zeus, stood ready, at the god's side, to serve him food and drink. It's interesting too to note that the boy's father was keep informed of each stage of his son's abduction and, indeed, his great wish was to have a son who would be handsome enough to attract a suitable suitor--one influential enough to give the boy a boost into the better classes, knowing full well that his boy would be the object of sexual passion, as the father had himself been as a boy.

Boys in Greece were free to choose their suitors, while the boys' sisters had to comply with their father's wishes, wishes based on political and economic advantages. The boys received continual gifts and tender attention from their lovers, the girls were paid for and sent to the kitchen or the bed according to their husband's needs. Girls remained virgin until marriage and remained loyal to their husbands, boys could have as many relationships with other boys and men as they wished, each serving as a step upwards in the boys' advancement through society. As related, the same was true for Hadrian who sought influence with Trajan by plowing the buttocks of the emperor's consorts, and the pages who had the greatest influence over the emperor. In Athens as well as in Rome, boys and their multiple lovers remained friends, often throughout their entire lives.

Prostitutes served as an alternate form of sexual outlet. Romans and Greeks had the choice of women, girls, men, boys and pleasuring themselves. The only difference was that Roman men could not have sex with other Roman men or women (other than one's own wife or husband), but only with foreigners, slaves and prostitutes--a rule certainly broken on occasion. And they had to be the top, in today's parlance, never the bottom. In Greece anything went down as normal and good, although throughout all time the penetrator has always been more respected than the penetrated. Prostitutes were looked down upon and Roman or Greek nobles thought to have sold their wares were tainted throughout the rest of their lives. Caesar himself never lived down the accusation, most probably true, that he was King Nicomedes' boy while ambassador to Bithynia (again, Antinous' birthplace). In Athens the politician Aeschines lost power when accused of having been a rent-boy in his youth.

As in relationships today, at that time too one could turn on one's lover. There is the example of Philip of Macedon, Alexander the Great's father. When Philip was a boy he was sent to Thebes and placed under the care of Pammenes, a great general and boy-lover who immediately reserved the young and willing prince for his bed. Pammenes is known for criticizing Nestor's role in the Trojan War because Nestor organized the men according to their country and not in groups of lovers and their belovèds, groups that would have fought to the death before letting down their loved-ones. No act was more valued than giving one's life for one's belovèd.

Later, when Philip was king of Macedon, his general Pausanias came to him with the complaint that he had been forcefully sodomized. Pausanias felt that he had the king's ear because they had been lovers when young. Pausanias claimed that he had had relations with a boy who killed himself when

Pausanias threw him over for another. The boy's former lover, a certain Attalus, decided to wreak vengeance on Pausanias by inviting him to a banquet, during which he forcefully raped Pausanias after getting him drunk (another version had Attalus aided by men who then took turns on Pausanias). Pausanias hoped that King Philip would avenge the outrage by killing Attalus, but Attalus was both an essential general in Philip's army and the father of Philip's wife. So to placate Pausanias, Philip named him to his personal guard, affording Pausanias the proximity he needed to drive a dagger into Philip's chest--thus opening the way for Philip's son, the Great Alexander. Pausanias, in turn, was cut down by Philip's guard.

In Plato's *Symposium* we learn that man-and-boy love was advantageous because no army could overcome the bond between lovers, and it worked in the favor of democracy because no despotic ruler was more powerful than the loyalty between men and their boys. We have the case of Harmodius and Aristogeiton. Hippias and Hipparchus were joint dictators in Athens. Hipparchus fancied Harmodius who refused his advances. To gain revenge, Hipparchus refused to let Harmodius' sister take part in the Panathenaea Games, accusing her of not being a virgin, a requirement. Harmodius and his lover Aristogeiton decided to rid Athens of the dictatorship and thusly redeem the honor of Harmodius' sister. With daggers hidden in their chitons, the boys fell on Hipparchus at the foot of the Acropolis, stabbing him to death. Hipparchus' guards immediately killed Harmodius and Aristogeiton was captured. While being tortured to reveal any coconspirators, Aristogeiton swore to tell the truth if Hippias would promise him clemency, sealed with a handshake. When Hippias complied, Aristogeiton laughed at his having shaken the hand of his own brother's murderer. Hippias, mad with fury, thrust his dagger into Aristogeiton's throat.

Plato claimed that the ideal nation would be based on lovers such as these, because no lover would ever dishonor his belovèd. To the contrary, he would do everything in his power to build him up, to educate him, to do for him all that was virtuous and good and honorable. All the great gods, all of them with the one exception of Ares, god of War, were lovers to their belovèds. (Ares was too unfeeling to appreciate tender friendships: he killed and maimed, and maddened men so they would take nursing babies from their mothers and dash their brains.)

Poets justified their love of boys by relating the story of how Zeus had abducted Ganymede:

Although boys can't be counted on to tell the exact truth about their first loves, Apollo claims that it was the beauty of Hyacinth that lured him into night games at the side of lads. Now, Hyacinth was a Spartan, born during the Mycenaean period, long before the laws of Lycurgus came into effect, making life in Sparta more difficult. After Lycurgus, boys were raised in the women's quarters until age seven, after which they were put in barracks and formed groups called herds ruled over by an older boy known as the boy-herder, who wielded a whip. They slept on reed beds, wore red cloaks, ate a sickening broth and were taught to forage for food because there was never enough in their communal messes. From age twelve the boys were free to choose older friends with whom they formed a sexual bond, friends who taught them what they needed to know about warfare and loyalty to the Spartan state. But when Hyacinth was born--before the laws of Lycurgus--Sparta was a city much like all the others in Greece, much like Athens, where boys Hyacinth's age could get a full education, had plenty to eat, and were free to hang around perfume and oil shops, and visit the barber to have their hair cared for and, when older, their nascent beards modishly trimmed.

Apollo would at times leave the stress of giving oracles at Delphi to sprawl out in the meadows of grass and flowers next to the Spartan river Eurotas. At the time Delphi was the most important site in Greece, just after Mount Olympus itself. Delphi. In the beginning the gods freed two high-flying eagles, one from the East, the other from the West. They met on the lofty crags of a great mountain that loomed over a jagged valley and the far-off port of Cirrha. Here was the sacred center of the universe; here was the spiritual navel of the Hellenes; here was Delphi, home of Apollo.

For Apollo had left his birthplace on Cycladic Delos to teach Man wisdom by revealing to him the future. Apollo traveled to the heights of Mount Parnassus where he destroyed the snake-like dragon, Python, its guardian. Then, with the help of the Muses and the consent of Mother Earth, he recruited sailors from a passing Cretan ship whom he made priests, and irreproachable villagers from the nearby village of Krissa whom he ordained priestesses, sometimes called Pythonesses in memory of the dragon. He built a temple, initiated the love of the arts, taught moderation and humaneness in all things, and himself tried to exemplify the virtuous life.

But as any lad knows, at times a boy needs more than moderation and virtue. At times he wants to let out all the stops. That's why Apollo chose the meadows around Eurotas. He loved clear streams and to bask in the sun and watch the Spartan boys, naked as the day, come down to swim and horse around. It made Apollo smile to see lads as frisky as yearlings, without a care in the world, while he had to continually divvy up oracles about which king was legitimate and which was not, which state would win a war if it crossed a certain river; and what the future held in store for this lass and her beau, or for that king and his kingdom, not to mention his obligation to adjudicate over poisonings, incests, murders and crucifixions. In a sense, the least of his worries was the wear and tear between his dad Zeus and ma Hera, and his brothers and sisters always and ever quarrelling.

The boy the others called Hyacinth was clearly better looking than the rest and better built, so unlike Apollo who was a bit hunky around the waist and whose buttocks were a shade large for a man. Hyacinth's were small, round and as solid as white marble. Of course, the sun, Apollo's brother Helios, had shaded the boy a tawny brown. The lad had long hair like Apollo, although the lad's fell over his shoulders, while Apollo's was sort of bunched up in a bun over his neck. Hyacinth and Apollo met when Hyacinth went to retrieve a discus he and his friends were throwing back and forth. Hyacinth was surprised to nearly stumble over Apollo, hidden in the high grass, but the god of Light had a nice warm smile and an easy way he'd learned over centuries on Earth, being Immortal and all. They fell into conversation and when his friends went home for dinner Hyacinth preferred to remain and talk with this man whose knowledge was greater than anyone the boy had ever known. Hyacinth soon left because he too was hungry but he returned day after day, his quest for knowledge insatiable. Apollo told stories about kingdoms the boy had never even heard of, and tales about kings and queens and battles and great warriors. They did physical exercises together and soon Apollo was in better shape than at any time in his life.

Lying with boys was normal intimacy for Hyacinth as the girls in Sparta were forced to remain locked up in their parent's homes and boys just naturally fell to giving each other a hand, and other things in preparation for later marriages. Hyacinth was especially attracted to Apollo because the god seemed to combine both sexes. His hips nearly resembled those of women and his breasts were much fuller than a Spartan boy's. In Sparta the lads were all slim-waisted and their pectorals were squared off and rock hard. So what happened was more of a surprise to Apollo than to the boy. They had met and now they loved, a new kind of experience for the otherwise very experienced god. In Greek and later Roman love, the man was always the penetrator. That much was clear. But Apollo being Apollo, the swordsman may have been, exceptionally, the young Hyacinth. At any rate, the god of Light was thrilled. Here was someone he could train with, run with, talk with, laugh with, a boy who introduced him to his friends, an intimacy that remained a closed intimacy between the two of them, but was hugely enlarged into a social event in which Apollo, Hyacinth and their friends were soon all laughing and playing and swimming and exchanging stories and knowledge. And Apollo loved the boys' laughter, so free and uninhibited and carefree and unbridled. While he and Hyacinth gave their youthful bodies in uncomplicated love, around them, hidden in the folds of grass, the other boys did the same, in pairs and in groups. Unrestrained, unruly, totally gratuitous, the end being a liberation of the demanding forces their bodies imposed on them since puberty, and then a race to the river to wash off. Hyacinth never pressured Apollo for something in exchange for the pleasure Apollo accorded him, because their release was mutual and thoroughly fulfilling and totally disinterested. Nor did the boy ever just lie there waiting for something to happen; theirs were two active virilities with never a second of monotony or boredom, something the god had not experienced with a mortal girl.

Hyacinth and Apollo

And then Apollo lost the most precious being to have ever graced his long, long existence. Apollo had been used to inflicting pain, as the time he'd skinned alive the mortal Marsyas when in a musical contest the poor earthling--claiming to be the better musician than Apollo--was outsmarted by the god who could play his lyre rightside-up or upside-down, while Marsyas could only make music through one end of his flute. Apollo and his fellow gods were used to raising those around them to incredible heights, before destroying them utterly, as they did Croesus, making him rich and powerful beyond dreams. Then he lost his empire to Cyrus, his precious son was gored by a boar, and his wife, when she learned of her boy's end, took her own life. Now it was the god's turn to suffer.

He and his precious belovèd had spent the morning mountain climbing, they'd swum and exercised, and were now throwing the discus, their bodies, Ovid tells us, were naked and sleek with oil, while their friends, stretched out in the high grass, were chatting as boys do, and applauding the god and the youth. Now, the West Wind had been spying on the couple and had decided that he too would try his hand at boy-love. But when Hyacinth paid him no mind, he became insanely jealous and caused the discus, thrown by Apollo, to fall to the ground where it rebounded and struck the forehead of the sweet youth. Hyacinth fell and where his blood fecundated the earth a bed of Hyacinth, rose-red flowers, sprang up. Apollo wailed the loss of his belovèd, arousing Zeus from his noonday sleep. He saw the beauty of the boy entwined in Apollo's arms, as the god of Light shed tears that marked the flowers with spots of white, and like a flower too the boy's head hung lifeless as though cut off at the stem. Thusly were Zeus' eyes opened to the wonder of the love of boys. He immediately took a wise decision: he too would find a companion to while away his days in mutual contentment, his nights in shared bliss, but as a first step, he would make the lad immortal.

He thusly abducted the Trojan youth Ganymede for his bed and--to ward off the smirks--dissimulated the fact by making him his cupbearer.

Soon Man followed suit. The Spartans made boy-love a virile pursuit in which lovers became valorous warriors, preferring death to the betrayal of their loved ones. The Athenians turned boy-love into a philosophical pastime in which, thanks to Eros, the intellectual and the physical were joined to make a new, self-sufficient man. In time the Trojan Aeneas would take the custom to the city he was destined to found on the banks of the Tiber. But this would be neither the virile nor intellectual fusion of body and soul known to the Greeks, but a monstrous, degenerative debauch of painted faces, effeminate bodies and fat slavering perverts.

Apollo had put all his science into reviving Hyacinth's still-warm body but its life had flitted away and already Hades had risen from the Underworld to claim what was his. Apollo stopped him with a glance, and womanish or not, Hades knew the look in those eyes and trembled, for he was confronted with the god of Light himself, who, next to Hermes, was Zeus' favorite son. So he crept back into the caverns of molten slime that awaited him. Apollo gently picked up the boy and carried him to the Elysian Fields, meadows and islands untouched by sorrow, a blessed land, the home of heroes and the deathless gods, a land free from toil, cradle of perpetual springs and shady groves and bubbling brooks, a cornucopia warmed by its own sun and illumined by its own stars--and eternally cooled by the West Wind, an obligation demanded by Apollo under pain of death.

And there Hyacinth lives, in Elysium, and in us, for the blood he shed nourished the sweet earth, the sweet earth that nourishes us so abundantly to this very day. (5)

As in Rome, the Greeks too were unaware of the concept of sexual orientation. Men quite simply did what they wanted to do (as the enlightened ones do to this day). Only the role in the act was of importance. In Rome and in Athens the penetrator was masculine, adult and of high social status; the penetrated was a youth or, if not, he was categorized as being effeminate or socially inferior. Not only did men share a sexual relationship with boys, they saw to it that boys were educated in the Greek way, meaning in the responsibilities that would be theirs in manhood. The period between the moment the man took a liking to a boy and the moment he quenched his desire, could be several weeks or months, giving the youth time to assure himself that the man had a genuine attachment for him that surpassed sexual lust. Normally the youth had some body hair, but cases of boys being appropriated at age 12 were not unknown.

Such was Patroclus' role with his belovèd Achilles: friend, teacher and protector, as related here: ''Both arranged their clothes. Achilles slipped into the bed the first, and then Patroclus. Patroclus found his place against Achilles' side, his leg gently draped over his belovèd's thighs. Did Patroclus foresee his coming fate, a fate he knew he held in common with others, as he held in common the happiness that filled his heart at this moment, a happiness that was his, but one that others had known and would know again, and that long after he had become dust? He put his arm under his beloved's head and leaned over him, silently searching the blue eyes. Finding his answer, he kissed the parted lips. He then moved his head back and with one breath blew out the oil lamp, bringing down night, a celestial curtain.'' (5)

In Rome the use of perfume and cosmetics and others forms of effeminacy were tolerated when they concerned youths, but not other men. Roman boys and men were allowed male-slave-sexual-partners as a way of discharging one's lust, an alternative form to pleasuring oneself. The male-slave-sexual-partner was generally replaced, sooner or later, by a wife. The slave would then cut his hair short and join the domain of the other slaves. A slave boy could be castrated to preserve a youthful aspect, as Nero had castrated Sporus before marrying him. Naturally, slaves could service their mistresses as well as their masters. As with Caesar (and King Nicomedes), Roman males often went through stages during which they evolved from being sexually passive to sexually active.

Same-sex marriages were not legally recognized in Rome. The aforementioned Juvenal criticized them because he felt that one day they would be legalized. Nero purportedly married two men, Pythagoras and Sporus, Nero the veiled bride, the men rewarded with a substantial dowry. Cicero accused Marc Antony of being a slut in his youth and married to Gaius Curio, one of many reasons Antony insisted on Cicero's death the moment Antony gained power. The exquisite Emperor Elagabalus is reported to have married his charioteer, Hierocles, and the athlete Zoticus. I like Elagabalus because he made no attempt to hide his true nature and because he used people and let people use him: stark naked, he would stand at the door of his palace or a tavern or the entrance to the baths and offer himself to all comers, out Messalina-ing Messalina. (According to David Bret in his book *Errol Flynn*, Flynn did the same thing, standing nude and fully erected in his studio dressing room, the door open, taking on anyone who would enter, girl or boy.) Elagabalus also had pimps sent to the far corners of the empire to bring him well-endowed boys, sailors being his specialty.

Elagabalus

Born in Syria, he became a priest of the god Elagabal (meaning god of the mountain--El-Gabal, or Baal). In Rome he raised the god higher even than Jupiter. In fact, he returned from Syria with the Black Stone, the most sacred object in the worship of Baal, and built the Elagaballium, a temple on the Palatine to honor it. To the disgust of Romans, cattle and sheep were sacrificed there at the dawn of every day, to please the new sun god, and senators were obliged to attend. During one yearly ceremony in honor of Elagabal he marched backwards, facing pure white horses drawing a chariot, perhaps winking at its driver, the well-known and well-hung Hierocles, a blond athlete he had married and whom he called his husband. The triumphal procession was in homage to the Black Stone's summer residence, outside the city. His second favorite was another athlete, Aurelius Zoticus, who was named Master of the Bedroom and whom he called, according to the *Augustan History*, his husband (see Sources concerning the *Augustan History*). In honor of his god, Elagabalus had himself circumcised, although after his death both the new religion and circumcision died a deserved death. He married five times, one of his wives being a Vestal Virgin, a flagrant disrespect for Roman law and an action that should have seen the Vestal buried alive and her ravisher put to death. One of his other wives had a husband he ordered killed so they could marry. Herodian (see Sources) claims that he was extremely good-looking, and also that he offered his physician "vast sums of money" to cut him a cunt--which the doctor sagely declined to do.

Elagabalus then decided to have himself castrated, which he changed at the last moment to the above-mentioned circumcision. Dio Cassius (see Sources) states that he loved to frequent whorehouses where he donned a wig and took on all comers.

He was only called Elagabalus after his death. During his reign he was Marcus Aurelius Antoninus Augustus.

Elagabalus became emperor at age 14, following the assassination of Caracalla, a bloodthirsty murderer responsible for thousands of deaths. While urinating at the roadside, a member of Caracalla's personal guard, Julius Martialis, whose brother Caracalla had had executed a few days before, ran him through with his sword. Caracalla was 29. Martialis was immediately shot dead by a Scythian archer. Caracalla was replaced by the head of the Imperial Guard, a man Elagabalus' vicious grandmother, Julia Maesa, ordered killed so that Elagabalus could take his place as emperor. As she was wealthy in the extreme, she had bought off the Guards. Julia Maesa's daughter--Elagabalus' mother--helped things along by claiming that she had had an affair with Caracalla, and that Elagabalus was Caracalla's son, making him heir to the throne. Both Julia Maesa and his mother became senators, the first women ever allowed in the senate (and the last). Around the same time that Elagabalus lost Caracalla, on whom it was said he had a huge crush, he lost his father and grandfather, both of whom he seemed to have dearly loved, all of which seemed to have been highly destabilizing for the adolescent boy.

Elagabalus' lifestyle could only make enemies within the senate and nobility, and disgust among Romans in general. His grandmother, the same who had put him on the throne, realizing her mistake in having him named emperor, conspired with her *second* daughter to have *her* son, Alexander Severus, age 13, replace Elagabalus. Elagabalus didn't know the details of the conspiracy but he did know that something was up and that Alexander was involved. As the bad blood between them became known, they were both summoned to the headquarters of the Imperial Guard in the hope that a solution could be found. Elagabalus, believing he still had the backing of his grandmother and her wealth, accepted to appear before the guard with

Alexander. He did so accompanied by his mother. On arrival the guards cheered Alexander, and Elagabalus, vexed, ordered the immediate execution of Alexander's followers. In response, the guard stripped both Elagabalus and his mother naked, decapitated them, dragged the remains through Rome and threw what was left into the Tiber. Elagabalus was 18.

Later, Alexander was himself killed by his guard at age 27 when he tried to buy off invading Germans instead of fighting them bravely as a Roman should.

Rapists were subject to death if they raped a woman, boy or man. Slaves, prostitutes and entertainers were public property, and as such couldn't be raped (even up to Shakespeare's time actors often rounded off their monthly earnings through prostitution). A man who was raped (anally or orally) was legally exempt from public stigma. It goes without saying that rape was the perfect vengeance, and according to some sources it occurred as often between men as it did between men and women among the Romans. When it happened to a Roman citizen it was thought to equal, in horror, parricide, the rape of a virgin or the robbing of a temple.

Augustus banned soldiers from marrying, a ban that held good for 200 years. Soldiers could not have sex among themselves in the same way that no Roman citizen could have sex with another Roman citizen outside of marriage. Many took mistresses and had children that they recognized after leaving the service. All turned to prostitutes of both sexes and gang rapes following military conquest--it was in fact a key perk. As with all other Roman citizens, a man was forbidden to lose his masculinity by allowing his body to be violated. The historian Polybius wrote that a soldier found guilty of being penetrated was clubbed to death. Plutarch recounts the story of the handsome recruit who was pursued by his commanding officer. He shunned the unwanted advances until the officer ordered him to, in effect, bend over. The recruit drew his sword and plunged it into the chest of the commander. Not only wasn't the recruit sentenced to death, the mandatory sentence, he was awarded the crown for bravery, the equivalent of today's medal of honor.

Women were expected to be modest and downgrade any pleasure they received during sex, which some men failed to believe, as we see in this quarrel between Zeus and his wife Hera:

"Will you pipe down?" commanded Zeus.

"And you. Have you no other words for your wife! Can you never greet me with the open arms of a loving husband?" sulked Hera.

"I have a reputation for being unloving and difficult because I don't accept being harassed by people like you. But if you'd make an effort to be civil with me, you would find me the most understanding of men."

"Is it civil, my husband, to abandon my bed as you do and spend your days in lustful pursuits?" moralized Hera. The goddess's pleated gown of white Cosan silk flowed in a sweeping, graceful arc from under her painted, uplifted breasts to her large, sandaled feet. "Should not a man be drawn to his wife by the links that bind them at the time of their marriage? Are they not to honor and obey, love and be faithful? How strange it is for you to talk of what is correct."

"I can no longer put up with your continual complaints," flared Zeus. 'All I want is a warm hearth with steaming ambrosia and a stout nectar, my pipe filled, my socks darned, and my favorite chair cleared of dogs. I ask no more than the most common of mortals. I know of mere peasants who live in greater comfort than I.

"But look what I provide you in return. I give you palaces, slaves, rule over the gods, a daily change of robes and sandals, dominions in Heaven and on Earth, plus islands, your own herds and flocks, rivers and lakes, not to speak of countless subjects and a personal Oracle. As for that snide little comment about our bed, don't forget that our honeymoon alone on Samos lasted three-hundred years. Each fortnight you're honored with my presence, and since the pleasures of the boudoir are far greater for women than for men, you enjoy much more satisfaction that I--my flirtations included."

"You're insane. Everyone knows that a man has more pleasure in love than a woman."

"Nonsense. The opposite is true. The proof is that men talk a great deal upon the subject when among themselves to compensate for the lack of the real thing. Whereas women--harlots excluded--keep quiet about it because they are satiated and because if men knew about the enjoyable time women have, they would all want to change their sex. Who would be left then to provide you with your play toys?''

''That's the most outrageous, the sickest thing I've ever heard. But wait. Would you like to put what you've said to a test?'' challenged Hera.

''Here you go scheming again. Can't you remain one minute without hatching some new plot?''

''This is no plot and anyway it's you who've asked for it,'' began defiant Hera. ''Listen: One day the mortal seer Teiresias came upon two serpents that were coupling and killed one of them, the female. As always happens in such cases, Teiresias was turned into a woman and spent seven years as such until one day she came upon two other serpents coupling and killed the male, becoming herself a man. He has therefore lived the life of a woman and a man and can tell us who is the receiver of the most pleasure. Would you agree to calling him?''

''I would indeed,'' accepted Great Father. ''Hermes! Hermes!'' From the orchard appeared a splendid youth.

''Yes, Father,'' said tender Hermes in dutiful compliance.

''Go to earth and bring back Teiresias,'' ordered Zeus.

''That's not necessary, Father,'' said the young lad. ''He's here himself. Athena has turned him into a woman for spying on her in her bath, and he's come to ask you to change him back.''

''Ye gods! *You* do it, and then bring him here,'' commanded quick-tempered Zeus.

''As you see, Husband, if it were so pleasurable to be a woman, why would Teiresias want to be turned back into a man?'' concluded self-satisfied Hera.

''That we'll find out right now. Here he comes.''

Teiresias, an old man with long, faded hair and an effeminate gait shuffled in. He wore a tattered, purple robe which trained on the floor as he came forward.

''Come here, Teiresias. My wife and I would be grateful if you could shed some light on a rather age-old problem: During ... uh

... the act of love, who has the most pleasure, the man or the woman?''

Hera and Zeus anxiously awaited the answer that was unforthcoming.

''Well, good man, don't leave us in the dark,'' prodded Zeus.

''Tell my husband what he wishes to know,'' urged Hera, leaning towards Teiresias, whose quivering lips were on the verge of parting.

''What am I to say?'' began frightened Teiresias, looking from the goddess's stern, sagging jowls to Eternal Father's craggy, once-handsome face. ''Which of you am I to obey? I'm sure that if I answer that it is men who have the most pleasure, I will receive blows from one of you; while if I answer that it is women, I shall be set upon by the other.''

''Have no fear, dear fellow,'' assured humane Father. ''I give you my word that I shall not harm you, and you know that the word of a man if his bond.''

''I'm certain one of you will become angry and take revenge upon me,'' sniffed Teiresias.

''Speak. No one will hurt you,'' cooed Hera, fingers crossed.

''If I knew which of you was for what...'' essayed Teiresias.

''No!' shouted Hera, knowing that Zeus' power would ensure him the vote. ''We want only the truth!''

''Would you repeat the question?'' quaked Teiresia.

''Of course...'' started Zeus.

''It's my turn!'' interrupted Hera. ''The question is: Who has the most pleasure during sex...''

''Mother!'' cried puritanical Father.

''...the *man* or the woman?''

''So as not to offend either of your godlinesses, let me answer with a little verse that you can interpret as you wish.''

''Oh, the coward,'' fumed Hera.

''He's been a woman too long,'' concluded Zeus. ''But say your verse. If it's too obscure we'll take it to one of the Oracles.''

''And it'll come back a dozen times less intelligible,' said Hera. 'But proceed. Tell us your little poem.''

''Timidly Teiresias began. ''If the parts of sexual pleasure he counted as ten, thrice three go to women, only one to men.''

"Ha, ha, ha," rejoiced Zeus.

"You mischievous scoundrel," raged Hera, and in her furious anger she blinded Teiresias by casting a baneful spell over him. She then stormed out of the room. (5)

CHAPTER NINE

≈ The Boy's World: Sects, Religion, Astrology, Superstition and Human Sacrifice ≈

The Romans borrowed the full panoply of Greek gods, and the mythology concerning the gods is of such import that I've called upon it whenever it can throw light on the past, the mythological past the Greeks knew and the mythological past the Romans adopted.

Confronting illness, death--especially that of children, loved ones and one's own demise--Man invented super powers as we, today, invent super heroes. Not a day has passed in the history of the world when one man or group of men has/have not massacred another in the name of some god, all because we are still unable to accept responsibility for our own lives, fates and destinies. We still live in the dark, and religious ceremony is nothing more than a talisman to ward off evil.

I've plunged into the study of the mysteries, astrology, superstitions, spells, and the likes during Hadrian's reign, but I keep coming up against walls that frustrate advancement. Ceremonies were not written down, and the little we do know doesn't square with what one historian or another says. The sad consequence of this ignorance is that we don't understand Hadrian's commitment to this rite or that mystical influence, which is of capital importance due to the fact that these influences most certainly motivated his interactions with Antinous, and, many believe, led directly to the boy's drowning.

Spells were of importance because if one could arm oneself with the property of the person one wished to cast a spell upon--nail or hair clippings, for example, available at a barbershop--one could maim or even kill an adversary. Or one could fashion a doll of wax representing the victim and do bodily harm by piercing it with needles.

Human sacrifice has been a tool used since the dawn of time. Hannibal, after seven years of fighting in Italy, made his way to the very gates of Rome. The alarm was such that the Romans resurrected a ritual dead for a hundred years: they sacrificed two men and two women, Gauls and Greeks, all four buried alive. Herodotus (see Sources) talks about the sacrifice of victims by the Athenians at the Acropolis during the second Greco-Persian war in 480 BC. Romans accused the Carthaginians of sacrificing infants, a question still being debated by historians. In the time of Livingston one African king sacrificed as many as 2,000 people a day when feeling ill, thanks to which he knew he would be restored.

Horoscopes were forbidden by Hadrian, except those he himself ordered or carried out, as he became an accomplished astrologer. Horoscopes done by others could give the date of an emperor's death, an encouragement to his enemies who felt safe in rising up against him when the forecasted moment came. They were therefore banned and those who cast them put to death.

Hadrian was also influenced by the story of Osiris and Isis. The ancient Egyptian myth was of importance because thanks to it a dead person could reach a pleasant afterlife. Because it was deemed unwise for Egyptian priests to put too many details in writing, what we know about Osiris and Isis varies widely from one ancient version to another. To start with, Osiris ruled Egypt with his queen Isis. He was murdered by Set, perhaps because he had slept with Set's wife. It seems that his body was cast into the Nile where Isis found it after much searching, her tears of mourning the reason why the Nile rises, flooding and fertilizing the fields around it. She had to carefully wrap the body to preserve it from decaying, an act which foresaw future mummification. When Osiris was at last made whole again, he and Isis had a son, Horus (a wondrous miracle as supposedly Isis found all of Osiris' body parts except his penis). Pharaohs hoped that they too, like Osiris, could be restored to life and eventually rule over the realm of the dead. As Antinous was drowned on the very day the Egyptians celebrated the story of Osiris, his death may have been a human sacrifice, say some historians, initiated by Hadrian, the goal of which was to preserve what remained of his health and extend what remained of his life. Trajan too had honored Osiris with votive offerings of wine, and Hadrian decorated his villa at Tibur with scenes from the lives of Isis and Osiris.

We know that Demeter and Dionysus played roles because in both cases stories concerning them centered around life, death and resurrection, but with the advent of Christianity--and Christ's rebirth--this form of afterlife faded in popularity. Christianity, however, could never replace Dionysian intoxicants, thanks to which inhibitions and social constraints were abolished, leading to--amidst frantic drum playing and voodoo-style dancing--what must have been among the most erotic orgies in history (8). Dionysus united with Apollo not only to have ascendancy over mankind through the gift of immortality, but also, due to Apollo's homoerotic inclinations, to ensure the power of men over women. Dionysus had been Zeus' love-child and when Zeus' wife Hera found out that he had again betrayed her, she had Dionysus frayed alive, torn to shreds, and boiled in a cauldron. It took all of Zeus' mother Rhea's art to bring Dionysus back to life, and then she only half succeeded. Like the vine Dionysus raised to the status of a cult, he too took on the aspect of death six long months of the year before sprouting horns and a head of hair full of vine leaves and creepers at the time of the summer solstice. He became the very symbol of Immortality. If he could be reborn, why couldn't Man? It was the hope of immortality that brought him worshippers. His cult spread throughout the land enclosed by Ocean, growing to such numbers that Zeus had been obliged to make place for Dionysus among the Ruling Twelve on Olympus.

As men's power over women grew, women's traditional roles as comforters and pacifiers, taking the edge off men's violent natures, pushing men to peace when their inner leanings cried out for revenge and war, ceased. In Sparta women's hair was cropped, and they dressed as boys, reduced to becoming the child bearers Apollo had envisioned. The men slept together in their own joint quarters, venturing out at night in packs to the women's barracks to rape their spouses. Stimulated by the moonlit view of their comrades, their buttocks rising and falling, the virile members thrusting and retreating, they found the erotic spur to procreate their race, so that later on there would be boys for their beds, and men to stand in honor of the commanders they would become.

Hadrian deeply appreciated Trajan's wife Plotina who was interested in the ideas of Epicurus, the Epicurean philosopher who urged calm and tranquility of character. Epicurus maintained that the gods were remote and ineffectual entities who cared nothing for humans. Death, according to him, resulted in the end of the body and the soul, which made fear of a vengeful hereafter ridiculous. A happy, peaceful life could be achieved through kindness and friendship, and by moderation of one's appetites. Many of Plotina's beliefs may have carried over into Hadrian's life. For example, he awarded his friends with banquets and made certain that three of them always accompanied him in his carriage. He visited his ill friends, one of whom was the philosopher Euphrates whom he allowed to drink hemlock when age and sickness were robbing him of his nobility as a whole man, a lesson for us today.

Hadrian even took advice from passersby. An old woman at a crossroads asked to speak with him. When he maintained that he was too busy to stop, she chastened him by shouting. "Then stop being emperor!" She was accorded her hearing.

The emperor was also influenced by the Stoics whose founder, Epictetus, taught the importance of self-control in overcoming destructive emotions. One must free oneself of anger, envy and jealousy and accept all men as equals, even slaves. Epictetus went on to write: "If I am alive at noon I shall eat heartily, but if I die before dinner I shall not complain, as I am only giving back what does not belong to me."

The Christians suffered largely because of the Jews who considered them heretics, and hardly surprising, too, given Jesus' contempt for the moneychangers in the Jewish temple. Like the Jews who have been blamed for committing unspeakable crimes throughout all history, the early Christians too were accused of crimes such as cannibalism, since they drank the blood and ate the body of Christ, and incest, as they called each other brother and sister. The early Christians, again like the Jews, didn't mix with non-Christians, and were therefore despised as arrogant and elitist, but an important difference between Jews and Christians was that the Jews, from time to time, had a country, while the Christians were just a dissident sect. The Romans felt that if their own gods were neglected due to the rising influence of the Christians, they would seek revenge by raining down misery and destruction on the people. Roman Christians turned away from the commonest of pleasures, like the slaughter in the gladiatorial ring, and they continually preached the end of the world, the best possible terminator of *joie de vivre* among the Romans--then as now the world's foremost hedonists.

Because the Christians kept to themselves and held meetings which were often secret and at night, they appeared dangerous. When Rome burned, Nero didn't hesitate to blame them and to sacrifice great numbers in order to turn suspicion away from himself. He had some Christians dressed in hides and hounded by dogs, others were crucified, some were burned at night to provide light (or so we're told by historians who were there). Christians could escape death by honoring the Roman gods; all that was needed was to make a sacrifice on a Roman alter; even a few grains offered to the gods could suffice. Those who refused were killed outright or thrown to the lions, to the immense pleasure of the crowds that hated them for their disrespect of Rome's gods. Even the usually wise Marcus Aurelius eventually turned against the Christians because he came to the conclusion that their unwillingness to honor Roman deities was surely the reason for every calamity that descended on the city, and Emperor Trajan resisted the Christians for fear that their peaceful nature might rub off on his legions, turning them into pacifists.

CHAPTER TEN

≈ The Boy's Deification ≈

Antinous was born into a Greek family in the small town of Claudiopolis, in the Roman province of Bithynia, a handsome nobody who died a prince, and has come down to us as a star even more famous than the very emperors of Rome, with possibly the few exceptions of Augustus, Caesar, Caligula and Nero. His inspired sculptor, an unknown genius, created the embodiment of masculine beauty, equaled only by Michelangelo's *David*. Antinous is of those boys of whom Musset wrote: *Voici une belle nuit qui passe.*

He was admitted into the Imperial court and sent to Rome where he learned Latin, poetry, history and the arts; his body was sculpted in the gymnasium; his mind by the best tutors of the age.

Antinous loved to hunt, perhaps even as much as Hadrian. Several historians testify to the truth of the story of Antinous hunting with Hadrian, in Egypt, just prior to his death. The aging emperor, in an attempt to impress the youth, took him on an expedition to track down a lion reported to have killed several people in the region. Seeing the lion, Hadrian deliberately just wounded it. The animal charged Antinous who, in his panic, lost his spear. Hadrian intervened, just in time to save his belovèd's life. Hadrian had always been noted for his courage, having broken his collarbone while single-handedly spearing a boar, and nearly losing his leg in another hunting adventure for which we have few details. In saving Antinous, Hadrian showed the courage of a man over that of a boy, as well as a man's power over life and death. Would he use that power, later, in order to prolong his own existence? Antinous spent 7 years at Hadrian's side (the mystical number mentioned in Chapter Two), much of which was dedicated to hunting--7 years, the lifespan of a hunting dog. Legend has it that where the lion's blood was shed, red lotus flowers sprang up, flowers the emperor offered Antinous, flowers that were soon to become his emblem and adorn his sarcophagus.

A blood-red lotus flower

Shorty after this incident, in Egypt, the emperor and Antinous boarded the imperial fleet and sailed to Heliopolis, home of the phoenix, a bird reborn from its own ashes, the ultimate representative of transformation and resurrection. Here Hadrian consulted with Pachrates, a sorcerer and caster of spells-cum-priest who had built his reputation for having magical powers thanks to his Egyptian heritage. After being well paid by the emperor to demonstrate the extent of his black arts, Pachrates chose a victim that took just two hours to die once Pachrates' spell--recited over a mortared paste of field mice, baboon excrement, goat fat and beetles--came to an end. Hadrian is thought to have paid handsomely for the recipe and accompanying incantation.

From Heliopolis, on their way to Hermopolis, the man and boy visited the pyramids and the Sphinx. At Hermopolis its yearly festival--celebrating the death and resurrection of Osiris, a celebration concomitant with the flooding of the Nile, the source of all wealth to ancient Egypt--was in full swing. The Nile had mysteriously failed to overflow its banks for two years running, and the people were threatened with starvation. The ceremony had thusly taken on a gravitas unknown in earlier years. The reader will remember that Hadrian had always been a fervent believer in the occult, the mysteries, the forecasts of soothsayers and fortunetellers--an interest that he had manifested even years before it had been predicted that he, the son of a simple senator, would one day lead the Roman world. The story of Osiris and Isis was of special importance because Osiris, after his death by drowning in the Nile, had been resurrected. He who had been cut into pieces by his enemy Set had been made whole again. Hadrian knew that in ancient times boys of great beauty were thrown into the Nile, a human sacrifice in memory of Osiris' martyrdom. The boys went willingly as they were led to believe that they too would be resurrected, and as Osiris, they too would become gods.

The manipulation of boys has been a constant throughout history. There is the example of Sinan, the head of a hashish cult called the Assassins, an organization capable of doing, in real life, what the godfather had done in film fiction with the horse's head placed stealthily between the director's legs. Both Richard Coeur de Lion and Saladin, the finest warriors the world had to offer at the time, were so terrified of him that they did everything in their power to placate the old man--bowing to his every wish and ultimatum. Boys were accepted into the cult very young, and when the moment came for them to be used as killers, they were drugged (*assassin* comes from the Arabic word *hashish*) and were then admitted into a garden where they found, upon awaking, fountains, wonderful food and all the girls their young bodies could accommodate. They were told that this was Paradise, and that if they were lucky enough to be killed during their mission, this is what awaited them in recompense. Sinan then sent them to perform various tasks, aimed at securing power and wealth for Sinan himself.

It is believed that Hadrian had cast his own horoscope and found nothing but impending disaster, a far cry from the horoscope predicting he would become emperor. His travels had tired him; he was becoming old; he suffered from bodily aches, especially his legs that were not only racked with pain but seemed cast in iron; and from every corner of the empire unrest, revolts and other never-ending problems assaulted him. The Nile itself was suffering, as were the people scratching a living on its banks. Everything combined to bring out the morbid aspects of his personality. He knew he was dying, that he was losing his grip on the Roman world ... and on the boy at his side. He could see in his belovèd's eyes that he was not the virile man who had fought his way to power, had led armies, had governed wisely and generously: he saw instead the ageing head that could no longer inspire love--and it was unacceptable. Yet he chose not to destroy himself, he chose--perhaps--to destroy the vital living beauty he contemplated, unquenchingly, at his side.

For this kind of spell to work Antinous had to be in agreement, he had to go to his death willingly. Free will was essential, and even the Devil himself has no control over a man until he is accorded such control, through free will, which, in the case of a man's soul, demands that he sign it over to the Prince of Darkness (called, in French, *Le Malin*--The Wily One). Had Hadrian used his years of experience to convince the boy that he, Hadrian, was at the end of his tether, and that without him the Roman empire, assaulted from all parts, would founder, bringing misery to countless millions? Did Hadrian believe that the boy's sacrifice would cure his ailments and perhaps even prolong his life? Had Antinous undertaken the voyage to the oracle of Siwa to ask for confirmation from the gods? This is the story I had recounted to my French lover, that the oracle had promised that each year the boy would have lived would be added to the life of the emperor. I told my belovèd nothing about Hadrian's other motives because, at the time, I was ignorant of them all. I had also told him that a thousand statues were raised in the boy's honor: in this I was mistaken, as over two thousand various statues, steles and bas-reliefs--not counting innumerable coins--have come to light. I told him that a thousand cities had been built in his memory: in this I erred, although countless temples, shrines and sanctuaries were erected.

We do know that the body, as beautiful as ever even in death (as the ancients claimed), was brought to the surface of the Nile in a fish net. The emperor was informed that the boy had certainly fallen from a bark while fishing. There was no mention of suicide, none concerning human sacrifice. The local priests maintained that traditionally all beautiful boys drowned in the Nile became gods, and indeed on the night of Antinous' disappearance the emperor had seen a star rise from the river and ensconce itself in the heavens where it was embraced by the other stars, among whom were Patroclus and Achilles, Harmodius and Aristogeiton, Alexander and Hesphaestion, Leonidas' 300 and the Theban Sacred Band (9). The priests begged for the honor of establishing a city in memory of the new god, a city called Antinoupolis.

Hadrian had it populated by Greek families and army veterans, offering the new inhabitants tax breaks, an assured food supply and other privileges. A new festival, the Antinoeia, was founded in his lover's memory. It included footraces, wrestling, boxing, chariot races, swimming and rowing, all performed by local ephebes. The prize was, naturally, a garland of red lotus flowers.

Hadrian--as Pontifex Maximus, High Priest of Rome--then ordered the deification of his friend, an unthinkable act as no other king or emperor--or even the Olympian gods--had ever dared to so honored what was, all in all, a boyfriend.

Alexander, too, had wished for his lover Hephaestion to be deified. He too had sent to Siwa for advice. The oracle declared that Hephaestion could not be worshipped as a god, but as a divine hero, news reported to have pleased Alexander. At the funeral of Patroclus Achilles himself had passed behind the kneeling bodies of twelve noble Trojan captives and had personally slit each of their throats, pushing the bodies into the funeral pyre of his lover.

This scene preceded Patroclus' martyrdom: Now Zeus turned his attention to Patroclus who had nearly reached the ships. He caused the Earth to shake and the mountains to explode in fire. The sun was blackened and the sea poured onto the beaches to douse the burning boats. Trojans and Greeks fell to their knees in awe and fear, each man with a fast prayer to Zeus-Savior on his lips. Only Patroclus was undaunted. Enveloped in light and with a bloodcurdling war cry resounding from his high-plumed helmet, he led the Myrmidons in attack. The Trojans mistook him for the mighty Achilles and scampered in full panic to the safety of Troy's walls. Father Zeus took pride in the noble Patroclus, and held his scales of Justice up for all the gods to witness his immutable decision to make Achilles' courageous friend the day's victor. How great, then, was his own deception when he saw the scales tip slowly but immutably downward in opposition to Achilles' companion. It suddenly became clear to Zeus that above glorious life, with all awesome beauty and heartrending disappointment, hovered motherly Clotho, Aunt Lachesis and grandmotherly Atropos, spinning, measuring and snipping; and not even Zeus had sway over their eternal labor.

The Fates chose Apollo as the carrier of death. The god of Light stopped Patroclus with a mighty shove as he was scaling Troy's walls. Patroclus hit the ground, shattering Achilles' spear and breaking the shield. He tried to regain his feet but Apollo gave him a slap that sent him sprawling back into the trodden dust. Still again the young prince sought to rise, but in vain. Apollo gave him one last shove that drove him clear of his fighting comrades and knocked the golden helmet from his stunned head. The boy's matter hair lay in ripples over his brow, and sweat blurred his half-closed eyes. Numbly he pushed himself to his hands and knees, but the blows from the immortal god had overwhelmed him.

Never again would he ride by Achilles' side, or listen for his friend's familiar steps coming up the beach, or hold him when fear swept his restive dreams. Already Death was ascending to claim the body, still warm and unmarked. Death regretted the work the Fates had dealt him, yet his role was not the worst: for it was not he, nor Man, nor the Immortals, nor Helios, nor any living thing that would see Patroclus lose his beauty and fall into dust: the final witness would be the still, solitary, anonymous grave.

Patroclus tried to rise; Death drew nearer; and Hector broke away from the entangled pack and approached the prince on running feet, his spear poised tightly against his side. Patroclus turned his chest and arched his body towards the blurred warmth of the midday sun which enclosed his head in a halo, his arms outstretched as if to welcome Achilles, not the quickly advancing Trojan. And it was then, on his knees, his body open to the sun and his friend, that Hector planted his spear in the taut muscles of the abdomen, at the place where he had first received precious life.

Nestor had Patroclus' corpse taken to the enclosure of waist-high stalks that surrounded the old king's tent. A group of servant maidens washed and oiled his skin, rinsed and combed his hair, dressed him in a white tunic and wrapped him in a wool sheet. The maidens had done what they could in the absence of his natural warmth, and the sweetness of his breath and the fragrance of his skin.

Odysseus was sent to the verdant lap of Mount Ida with a large detail to bring back logs for a funeral pyre. The trees were rapidly felled, branched and dragged back behind the soldiers' horses.

On a gently sloping plain behind the shore Aias and Teucer supervised the digging of a shallow pit in which the funeral pyre was to be raised and in which the offerings were to be burned. Agamemnon had given himself the job of getting together the sacrifice. He had requisitioned jars of honey, vine and oil; sheep, cattle and a covey of partridges; four horses, one of which had belonged to Patroclus; and two of Patroclus' hounds. Twelve Trojan captives were also to be slain.

Menelaus supervised the building of the pyre. The logs were placed in the shallow pit and crisscrossed to form a giant square the length and width of a ship. On the top, ten feet from the earth, a platform was built of planks.

From the heights of Olympus the Ruling Twelve descended on joyless clouds to the plain of Troy where they hung suspended in the darkened sky high above the site. The Winds, the Furies and the Planets joined them, as did Night, Day and Mother Earth; the Fates, the Cyclopes and the Dactyls; plus uncountable other lesser gods like the Stars, Moon and, alas!, Death.

Looking down on the plain that was wrapped in a warm blanket of autumn orange and gold, they saw the funeral procession drawing near the pyre.

The men marched slowly, each step in time to the haunting beat of the soldiers' swords striking against their shields. The Myrmidons led the procession. Six abreast and four hundred deep, they were dressed in full battle regalia. Patroclus was carried gently on the shoulders of Agamemnon, Odysseus, Diomedes, Idomeneus, Nestor, Calchas, Aias and Menelaus. Achilles led the Myrmidons. The rest of the troops took up the rear, forming a line a mile long.

From Troy's walls watched Priam, Hecabe, Antenor, Eiphobus, Helen and … Paris. Did it ever occur to the young fool that it was he the agent of such misery?

At the pyre, Achilles gave his eternal farewell to Patroclus. He did it simply, respecting even in death his lover's modesty. The corpse was lifted onto the platform. Below, into the gutters between the edge of the pit and the logs, the animals were sacrificed, the jars of food, oil and wine were emptied and the captured Trojans were condemned to die. Each of the twelve was on his knees facing the logs. Each had his hands roped behind his back. All waited their turn as Achilles himself passed behind, pushed his knee into their spines, pulled back their heads by the hair, and slit their throats with Patroclus' own dagger. Their lives, valiant manhood and beauty ebbed rapidly down their chests and formed puddles where they fell after being shoved into the pit. All the gods looked on sadly except Death, who was busy flittering from one victim to the next.

Then came the soldiers, each throwing in a gift or libation. Finally Achilles stood alone before the pyre with Antilochos to his right. He took Patroclus' dagger and cut off a sprig of his own hair. He climbed to the platform and laid it in Patroclus' folded hands. Antilochos stepped forward and handed Achilles a torch that he immediately threw into the straw between the logs. The Winds blew down from the clouds to help the fire get a sure start. Moments later it was a roaring blaze and in Hades, Patroclus, free at last, crossed over the Styx and onto the Elysian Fields. (5)

Proclamations of Antinous' deification were sent to the far corners of the world, and even the Roman Senate acquiesced--but then, they had also allowed Caligula to make his horse Incitatus a senator (a story, I rapidly hasten to add, that many historians doubt). The Greeks, who had mingled with the gods since the beginning of time, had no difficulty in accepting Antinous into the Olympian godhead. Only Cynics (of which, in Rome and Athens, there were many) cynically concluded that the acceptance of Antinous as a god by Athenians had something to do with Hadrian's subsequent decision to award the Greeks money subventions and stable food supplies. The boy's fame spread far and fast, fueled by peoples who, like the Greeks, had found a way to the emperor's heart and pocketbook. Some conversions to the cult of Antinous, in some localities eager for personal gain, were instantly accomplished by replacing the faces on existing statues with Antinous' image.

Having gained immortality by drowning in the Nile, only Egyptian priests could handle the body which they cleansed, enveloped in the rarest tissues and reduced to ashes. The immortal remains were sent to Hadrian's villa at Tibur where the emperor build two shrines, one facing the other, with an obelisk between them that recounted the deification of his friend and his transformation into the joint-god Osiris-Antinous.

There is still another aspect of the story that must be broached. A bas-relief has come to light showing Hadrian and Antinous on a hunting expedition. The Bithynian youth is shown as a strong young man with sideburns descending his cheeks. There is nothing of the boy of old. Rather, one imagines a youth on the threshold of becoming a man. As a Hellenist, Hadrian's desire was aimed at boys from age 14 onwards, whose cheeks, both facial and backside, were hairless, the penetration of which was easy due to the willing access that was permitted when one was young, but became less desirable as a boy reached manhood. A boy could be educated, influenced and manipulated; a young man resisted the beguiling maneuvers of a lover whose chief goal was the fulfillment of his lust. The natural result would have been for Hadrian to have taken on another; the natural result would have been for Antinous to have molted from belovèd to lover, from passive to active, from penetrated to penetrator, a man who would have found a boy for himself. In a perfect world he and the emperor would have remained friends, and Antinous would have become an advisor and continued as one hunting companion among others. But were the boy not to accept such an evolution, he may have literally decided to drown his sorrows. As one could not become a god if he committed suicide, the death was masked as an accident. Hadrian had no part in any of it, except for having--perhaps--flirted rather openly with younger boys, leading Antinous to believe that his time at the emperor's side was drawing to a close.

Hadrian is said to have cried like a baby, to the extreme embarrassment of those around him. The tears were certainly a genuine result of anguish, some for Antinous, *perhaps* most for himself as he became immediately aware that his physical ills had in no way been alleviated. He was as old and crippled as ever, but in addition he was now alone.

The historian Cassius Dio, who was nearly contemporary to Hadrian and Antinous, wrote: ''The boy was said to have fallen into the Nile, or, in truth, to have been offered as a human sacrifice. While still young Hadrian had fallen under the spell of soothsayers, fortunetellers, astronomers, augurs and the like and was willing to try all sorts of new spells and incantations. Perhaps he did so to bestow immortality on his belovèd, or perhaps to accomplish the ends he himself had in mind. What Hadrian did he did for love, or because the boy had voluntarily undertaken the ultimate sacrifice for him.''

The historian Aurelius Victor had written a short history of Rome, from the great Augustus to Constantius II. He claimed that Hadrian was known for debauching youths, the most exciting of which had been Antinous, for whom he burned with passion. ''Hadrian had wished to extend his lifespan by any means and had found the answer in charlatans who promised him immortality if a boy of supreme beauty would sacrifice himself, in the Nile, the source of immortality since the drowning of Osiris.'' One thing was for certain: as with Achilles and Patroclus, Antinous would not know the ravages of demeaning age. He died young and beautiful, and as such he will remain until the end of time.

Three views of the Antinoeion.
Recent excavations at Tibur have revealed the remains of a sanctuary dedicated to Antinous, the Antinoeion, two semi-circular temples facing each other, in the center of which was an

obelisk that Hadrian had sculpted in Egypt immediately after Antinous' death, and brought to Rome by boat. The obelisk recounts the martyrdom of Antinous, his resurrection and deification as Osirantinous. The obelisk is now located in the Pincian Hill Gardens.

Antinous' obelisk

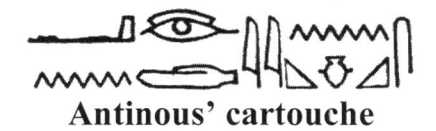

Antinous' cartouche

CHAPTER ELEVEN

≈ The Aftermath ≈

It hadn't taken Antinous' death for the emperor to contemplate his own end. Long before, he had ordered the building of an immense mausoleum destined to house his ashes, erected on the right bank of the Tiber. It was cylindrical in form with a garden on the top and a golden chariot drawn by four horses abreast, an emulation of that used by the gods. It remains today, without the horses, a splendid survivor--along with Hadrian's Pantheon--of the ancient world.

His health declined, due to Antinous' death or not will never be known. It is known that he had suffered from severe nosebleeds and skin rashes, red and painful, especially attacking his legs.

As mentioned, Hadrian traveled through Gaul to Britannia to Spain, northern Africa, Libya and on to the Euphrates, the Black Sea, Anatolia and Pontus. He went to Troy to pay his respects--as had Alexander the Great--to the city where Aeneas, the founder of Rome, had been born. In Aeneas' time trees lined the gently flowing Scamander that meandered serenely past the citadel and across the great plain of Troy on its way to time gray sea. Wild flowers bloomed along its banks and in profusion over the long-uncultivated sod. There were fragrant roses, the gift of Aphrodite; yellow fennel, used as a chalice by Prometheus to retain his gift of fire for Man; white petals of virginal narcissus; pink cyclamens; faint-blue capers; purple anemones; white daisies; and brittle stalks of pinkish asphodel, the meager flower of the dead. There were groves of apples, pears, cherries and plums, and the palm, whose fronds athletes carried as a symbol of their victories. The poplar grew--its twin-colored leaves represented hopeless Hades on the dark-green underside and the promising present on its silvery surface. It was also worn by athletes, as was the laurel, dear to Apollo ever since the mountain nymph Daphne changed herself into its evergreen branches to escape his embrace. Fig trees and myrtle bushes abounded. There were vines sacred to Dionysus and olive trees that gave precious oil. Violets--hated by Persephone who was innocently picking them when carried off by Hades to the Underworld--flourished in dark spots, as did the poppy, producer of opium, nightshade, from which strychnine was extracted, and the equally deadly hemlock. (5)

Aeneas was the love child of Aphrodite and a Trojan prince. She had given Aeneas godly horses that the Greek Diomedes, during the Trojan War, had captured. Apollo came to free them, giving Diomedes, at the same time, a lesson on boy-love: "Apollo descended just in time to see Diomedes make off with Aeneas' immortal chargers, the very same that Zeus had given to Troy ages before in exchange for the handsome Trojan youth Ganymede, who now served as Eternal Father's cupbearer and bedmate. Apollo reined in the steeds and shouted a warning to fearless Diomedes that if he meddled in the mysterious ways of the gods another time, he would be dispatched at once to the vilest depths of hated Tartarus. 'You're playing with fire, Diomedes, when you interfere with us Immortals and our godly gifts to Man. Now, these horses here were given to Tros, the founder of Phrygia's legendary town, in exchange for his son, a beauty if there ever was one. You probably know that Almighty Father learned the love of boys from me. He saw the way I was carrying on with Hyacinth. Now, Hyacinth was a Spartan lad who would put even Helen to shame. Mountain bred and cornbread fed, rosy checked and brawnily muscled, he was fancied by the West Wind too, but Hyacinth wouldn't give him a tumble. So in revenge the Wind caught one of Hyacinth's discuses in mid-air and flung it back, striking him on his curl-graced temple. I put up such a lament when I saw my friend lifeless that Zeus came to see what was going on. I told him about Hyacinth and Father went off to try his hand at boy-love. He wasn't long in finding Ganymede, and he was a hell-of-a-lot smarter than me: he made the lad immortal, thereby freeing him from the ravages of old age and fatal accidents. So, hand over those horses and get back to your work of killing men.' " (5)

During Hadrian's travels he hunted, bareheaded in even the worst weather, and always forsook wine before the hunt. He took care of government business in such detail as to be micromanaging. He made sure that the countries he passed through paid their taxes, contributed to the well-being of his armies, carried out his building projects and provided for the needs of Italy. Along the way he built aqueducts, roads, temples and government buildings. At Cyzicus he ordered the completion of a temple to Zeus, begun three hundred years earlier. At Rhodes he rebuilt the statue to the great god Helios (the greatest of them all, as we known, for he is the sun, without whom there would be no life on earth). Toppled by an earthquake years before his visit, it would fall again, after Hadrian's departure, for the same reason. In grateful thanks cities were named after him, the first being Carthage itself, renamed Hadrianopolis. Those in the know organized choruses of young men to sing his praises, events that stirred the emperor.

He went to Egypt, a Roman province since the defeat and suicides of Antony and Cleopatra. It was here, on the beach, that Pompey the Great had been beheaded, to the displeasure of Caesar (10).

He visited Sparta where boys, to show their courage, were still whipped, as they had been in more ancient times, their broad handsome backs crimson with blood, the onlookers, including the emperor, deeply aroused. In ancient times, in other backwaters of Greece, cannibalism, in the name of Cronus-Imbiber-of-Boys, persisted. Even in the more civilized regions of the Peloponnesus, especially around the Taygetus Mountains and especially at Sparta, boy sacrifices had given way to less loathsome although equally sinister rites. Boys were bound to an altar and flogged until their blood splattered the marble surface in symbolism of the earlier human sacrifices. Because the whippings were in honor of the god, the participating boys vied with each other to see which of them could accept the greater suffering without loss of face, and shed the most blood without loss of life. The frenzy of their zealotry, aided by the hallucinogens they drank to make the pain bearable, produced an erotic arousal of frenetic intensity. The resulting ejaculations, mixed with the streams of blood, came to symbolize the fecundity of the people, and the fertility of their lands. Ceremonies such as this, along with cannibalism, had disappeared ages before the arrival of Hadrian (3).

In Thebes Hadrian wrote a poem in the glory of Epaminondas, the leader of the sacrificed Sacred Band. He honored the inhabitants of Peloponnesian Mantinea who had founded Claudiopolis, the birthplace of Antinous. He visited the home of his hero, Xenophon, near Olympia. Not only did he visit cities but even villages could count on his bringing new water supplies, additional food, public works, theaters and entertaining games. He inspected garrisons and forts, abolishing some, establishing others. He investigated everything, weapons, trenches and ramparts. He made sure the ranks were getting good food and correct shelter, and that the officers were treating the men well and were not themselves living in unseemly comfort. He insisted on strict discipline and projects that kept the men busy around the clock.

He went on to Delphi where he climbed the Sacred Way, a narrow path that zigzagged up the steep mountain slope to Apollo's temple. It was lined on the mountainside by small marble temples, statues of gods and heroes, kings and divine animals, clumps of pines and cypresses, as well as olive and almond trees full of singing birds and chirping crickets. From high up Hadrian looked out over valleys and plains to the endless sea that sparkled in the distance. The mid-morning light was green, a mixture of the raging sun and the azure shadows cast by mountains and gorges, peaceful groves and tranquil glens. The beautiful walk to the temple was a spiritual preparation for his presentation before the god.

When he reached Apollo's magnificent sanctuary with its giant columns and sculptured front, temple priests came to greet him and familiarize him with the preparatory rites. He was taken to Apollo's altar where a sacrificial goat stood waiting. The priests instructed him to douse the animal with cold water. The goat immediately began to shiver, the infallible sign that Apollo was within his temple and willing to answer the suppliant's questions. The goat was sacrificed and the fat, inners and bones, along with wine and laurel leaves sacred to Apollo, were burned in offering to the god.

Hadrian was then admitted into the presence of the Pythoness. In respect for him as emperor of the Romans, he was allowed to sit on a stool.

We don't know the content of what the Pythoness revealed, but we do know that from there he traveled to Mount Etna, from the summit of which he viewed the rising of Helios.

Around this time the Jews again revolted. As I wrote earlier, Tiberius, Caligula and Nero were perhaps pustules on Augustus' ass, but in Nero's case, at least, some terrible things took place concerning the Jews which now concern this narrative. In 66 AD violence broke out when Greeks sacrificed birds in front of a synagogue. Because the Romans seemed to favor the Greeks and because they made the Jews pay what the Jews considered unjust taxation by the Romans, the Temple in Jerusalem ceased praying for the well-being of the emperor and stopped paying taxes. The

Romans entered the Temple and took the money they claimed was owed them. The Jews rebelled and the Romans were chased from the city. Massacres took place around Judea, involving hundreds of Romans and, due to Roman arms and skill, thousands of Jews. Nero expedited Vespasian, accompanied by his son Titus, to the scene. Titus raised a wall around the wall of Jerusalem which attained the same height. Anyone trying to escape from the city was caught between the two walls, taken to the summit of the Roman wall, and crucified in full view of the city inhabitants-- some say as many as 500 crucifixions took place daily. Zealots within the city, a Jewish sect that fostered violence and rebellion, burned the food supply an incentive to make the less violent majority fight. Titus added to the plight of the Jews by allowing Jews to enter the city, putting greater pressure on the food and water supply, but not allowing them to leave. For seven months Jewish men and women, perhaps a million within the walls, fought for survival, but eventually the walls were breached and Titus' men entered. The Temple caught fire, some historians say accidently as Titus wanted to convert it into a Roman pantheon, and the city sacked. Those who were not slaughtered were sold into slavery. A million Jews may have died during the revolt, most perhaps from dysentery and other diseases.

Before the revolt and the fall of Jerusalem, a group of Jews known as the Sicarii had overcome a Roman garrison on the top of Masada, a very high mesa. The Sicarii were an even more radical splinter group of the Zealots, and favored murder by dagger. They are said to have butchered thousands of their own people, women as well as children, who refused to obey their commands, and during the seizure of Jerusalem by Titus they had assassinated many men who had not fought with adequate ardor. Those who escaped the destruction of the Temple withdrew to Masada, followed by the Romans who built a ramp to reach the walls at the top of the mesa, walls they breached. The Sicarii committed mass suicide, one source forwarding the number as having been 960.

Hadrian, on his visit to Jerusalem, promised to rebuild the Temple and he did so, but dedicated it, on construction, to Jupiter Capitolinus and to himself. Hadrian also prohibited circumcision, considered a form of ungainly mutilation. Taxation was again imposed, but taxes levied on the Jews were now to pay for the upkeep of Jupiter's temple. The Jews again rebelled, but unlike former times, now they had a charismatic leader, one Bar Kokhba, of whom a respected rabbi said, "This is the Messiah". Kokhba's solution to uniting all of Judea was simple: like the Sicarii he massacred those who disagreed with him. Hadrian pursued him with twelve legions, and although Hadrian's losses were at first very heavy, his men, many imported from war duty in Germany, gained the upper hand. Victory came after three years of fighting, during which perhaps 600,000 Jew were killed. Prisoners were auctioned off, and so great were their numbers that they cost less than a horse. Hadrian had the Torah publically burned on the Temple Mount and Jews were no longer allowed in Jerusalem.

Hadrian had put Julius Severus, his troubleshooter, in charge of the war against the Jews. Severus' technique was never to attack his opponents openly but to intercept small groups. He confined the enemy in their cities, depriving them of food, and thusly, slowly, with little danger to his own men, starved, exhausted and exterminated them.

What had begun with Nero and had gone forward with Trajan ended with Hadrian. The Jews, eternally discontented, would never again pose a problem to the Romans.

CHAPTER TWELVE

≈ Hadrian's Successors ≈

Hadrian caught everyone by surprise when he named Lucius Aelius Caesar as his successor. Some historians believe that his only qualification was his beauty, and although he preferred women he is believed to have followed Antinous as Hadrian's lover. But Lucius suffered from tuberculosis and spat up blood, so ill he couldn't go before the Senate where one traditionally offered one's thanks for being adopted by an emperor. In fact, he rapidly dropped dead.

Lucius Aelius

Hadrian's second choice for adoption, just prior to his death, was Antonius Pius (the Pius, "pious", was added subsequently when he deified Hadrian against the wishes of most senators). Hadrian stipulated that Antonius adopt the son of his wife's brother, Marcus Aurelius, as well as Lucius Verus, the emperor's long-time favorite. Hadrian had known the child Lucius Verus since his birth because the boy's father, a very wealthy man of Spanish descent, had been a friend of Hadrian. Hadrian was attracted to this particular enfant thanks to his solemn nature and the fact that the child never told lies, the reason why Hadrian nicknamed him Verissimus, the most truthful. In this way Hadrian hoped to have nominated three emperors in a row, first Antonius, who was old, followed by Marcus Aurelius, and finally Lucius Verus who was much younger than the two others.

Lucius Verus and Marcus Aurelius

But Antonius' reign turned out to be extremely long, and the most peaceful in Roman history. He died of old age at 75. Marcus Aurelius became emperor and insisted that Lucius Verus be named co-emperor. Some historians believe he did this to honor Hadrian's request that both he, Marcus, and Lucius reign together, the reason why he had obliged Antonius to adopt them both. Other historians think that Marcus wanted to emulate the Spartans whom he admired, as they too had had a system of joint kings, one who remain in Sparta during time of war while the other took to the battlefield (3).

We all know of the brats that we love to hate. Lucius Verus was the opposite: he was the guy everyone loved to love. In looks, when a child, he could only be described as adorable, and in personality he was the charming kid everyone wanted to hug. His beauty and charm would take him far, beginning with Hadrian himself who had more than avuncular love for the boy. Proud of his looks, Lucius put gold in his hair to highlight it. He too loved young boys and men (Hadrian assumed to having been the first of many to follow), and when not spending his time in debauchery, he gambled. An inveterate tavern crawler, he enjoyed fighting and often returned home at dawn covered with bruises. He had a racetrack and spoiled his horses with raisons and nuts. His banquets cost a fortune, orgies during which the numerous young waiters were made available to older participants. In contrast,

Marcus Aurelius' palatial home was reserved for philosophers and intellectuals. Marcus, in honor of the Stoics, shaved his head, while Lucius let his hair grow long and wild. Lucius tried to corrupt the co-emperor by inviting him to his palace where Marcus could participate in his soirées. Marcus came, but did government work during the day and slept at night.

Marcus and Lucius offered a bounty of 20,000 sesterces to each soldier (and more to officers) when they came to power, twice the normal sum. The legions replied by swearing an oath to defend both to the death. To seal the bond between them, Marcus insisted that Lucius marry his daughter Annia Lucilla. (When Lucius died Annia was married off to a certain Quintianus whom she disliked because he was twice her age and not of noble rank. When Marcus died Lucius' brother, Commodus, became emperor. Lucilla tried to poison him in order to place her husband on the throne. Commodus escaped death and exiled Lucilla to Capri where he had her executed the same year.)

Marcus and Lucius went to war with Germania, Parthia and Armenia. Marcus, hoping to curb Lucius' debauchery, sent him to Antioch, not knowing (as a Stoic he wouldn't necessary know) that Antioch was, at that time, as I've said, the world capitol of vice. Lucius spent his nights whoring and playing dice, and his days racing chariots. He went off to the Danube when war broke out and died during transit, perhaps of smallpox, perhaps simply from hereditary causes as nearly all male members of his family died young.

When Hadrian was asked by a friend why he had adopted Lucius, Hadrian answered: "Through a quirk of nature, I have not been permitted to have a son." Then remembering his friend Julius Fabio's who, at a dinner the night before, had said that he wished he could drown his own boy because of his effeminacy, Hadrian went on: "A natural son turns out to be whatever Heaven decrees, be he stupid or maimed or girlish, whereas in an adopted boy one can choose a sound body and mind."

Marcus went on to rule so well that he is known to us as one of the Five Good Emperors--Nerva, Trajan, Hadrian, Antoninus and Marcus--a term coined, in 1503, by none other than Niccolò Machiavelli. Marcus too had been born in Spain. His mother had been extremely wealthy and had taught him religious piety and simplicity. As a youth he wore a rough Greek cloak and slept on the ground until his mother coaxed him to adopt a bed. He spent his life studying philosophy and was, as said, a convinced Stoic. His character was described as being blameless and his life as being temperate.

The greatest challenge to Marcus' reign was posed by the general Avidius Cassius who had gained a name for himself during the Parthian War. Later he won praise during the Syrian campaign and was elevated to the Senate. He was proclaimed emperor when false rumors circulated concerning the death of Marcus, who at the time was in Germany. It's believed that Marcus' wife, Faustina, was in on the plot because she genuinely believed her husband was near death and she wanted Cassius to step in as a temporary emperor until her son Commodus, then only 13, could become emperor *à son tour*. Cassius was in a good position because he controlled seven legions, but when the Senate found out that Marcus was alive, they declared Cassius to be an enemy of the people. As Marcus had more legions than Cassius and as Cassius lacked sufficient public support, he withdrew to Egypt where a dissident soldier beheaded him. The head was sent to Marcus who ordered it buried (without looking at it, adds, primly, one historian).

He died at age 58 after having been ill and in weak physical condition all his life, although he may have been carried away by small pox or measles, which at one time killed 2,000 people a day in Rome, reaching a total of 5 million dead.

Hadrian's mausoleum.

Hadrian's mausoleum (known today as the Castel Sant'Angelo) was commissioned by Hadrian. His ashes were interred there a year after his death, along with those of his adopted son Lucius Aelius, named to succeed Hadrian but died just before the emperor. The remains of other emperors were placed in the mausoleum, the last Caracalla in 217. Hadrian also ordered the construction of the bridge leading to the mausoleum, the Pons Aelius.

≈ Hadrian's Deification ≈

When considering his succession, Hadrian had contemplated adopting his brother-in-law Lucius Servianus and Servianus' grandson Fuscus, thusly assuring two generations of emperors. Servianus had been told that during a banquet Hadrian had asked his guests to name ten men capable of taking the emperor's place at the time of his deification. He then paused and said, "No, not ten, only nine, for I already have one man in mind, Servianus." When Servianus learned that neither he nor his grandson would be adopted by Hadrian as a first step to their becoming emperors, he attempted to gain support for the physical removal of Hadrian. When the emperor found out, he had both men killed. Before dying Servianus asserted his innocence and prayed to the gods that when Hadrian's time came, "He will suffer so greatly that he will beg for death, but will be unable to find it." And this is precisely what happened.

His nosebleeds continued and his skin rashes, especially around the legs, became increasingly more painful, as did his legs in general. He attempted to bribe those around him to give him a sword or poison, as his own sword, kept under his pillow, had long since been removed. He pleaded with his slave and herculean hunting companion, Mastor, to knife him at a spot the emperor himself marked, in red, under his left nipple, the place that his physician, Hermogenes, had once indicated as the location of the heart. Mastor, through love or fear, fled in horror. Perhaps rightly so. When Richard Coeur de Lion was shot with an arrow by a young man whose father and brothers Richard had killed during a siege. Richard, impressed by the boy's courageous defiance, promised him not only his life but awarded him a sack of gold. Outside the king's tent Richard's men nonetheless fell upon the lad and skinned him alive.

The incongruity of the affair was that Hadrian could kill anyone in his empire, other than himself.

Hadrian was tired of suffering and of simply growing old, unable to hunt. In the uneventful years following the death of Antinous he knew that only his position as emperor, not his physical manliness, attracted the boys he so cherished. Hadrian grieved over the lad he had lost, but he knew that thanks to his early death there were truths the boy would never discover, truths that would have turned his boyish heart to stone, truths concerning the horrors of man's inhumanity to man, truths that would have taken gradual possession, cell by cell, of the young, still innocent beating in his valiant breast. Hadrian grieved too for himself, for his increasingly blurred sight and faulty hearing, for limbs that groaned beneath the body's weight, and for the worst ugliness of them all: the reflection of his shriveled self in younger eyes, eyes that recalled former times and earlier loves. Hadrian wondered at the enigma of humanity: ''Why did one mourn death--which was but eternal sleep--and not the coming of age, which was the veritable human night?''

As his end drew near, only the past became real--he went there often in mind and in dreams.

Hadrian was a Stoic, so at the end he was only rendering that which he had borrowed. He had lived sixty-two years. He had slept, marched, drilled and eaten with his troops, always maintaining discipline by keeping his men busy. He tried to keep the peace through strength. He had killed men--some out of jealousy, as the architect Apollodorus, others who deserved their fate, as had his brother-in-law Lucius Servianus and Servianus' grandson Fuscus. He had put limits on Proscription, Augustus and Marc Antony's way of extracting wealth from the rich by murdering them. He had kept his people fed and had eased their debts; had stopped many more wars than he had participated in and had instigated none; and he had loved what was certainly more than his share of mortal youths, thusly accepting the immutable nature of man by benefiting from the flesh of others while allowing others to benefit from his flesh. He had ameliorated the lives of countless peoples by bringing water, food, temples and games to their villages, towns and cities, and he had named two inheritors, one of whom went on to be nearly as great as the great Augustus himself, Marcus Aurelius, and during his last months he had written his autobiography, alas lost.

As the pain had increased, he had insisted that his doctor give him poison. When his insisting became too great, the doctor, Hermogenes, killed himself. The *Historia Augusta* gives this version of the events: ''Hadrian's entourage pleaded with him to put up with his ailments, and Antoninus stated that he could not help the emperor who had just adopted him because that would be akin to parricide. Antoninus wasn't supposed to know about Hadrian's attempts on his own life, and Hadrian ordered the man who had informed him to be killed, his life saved by Antoninus. Hadrian made out his will and then again tried to stab himself with a dagger that was forcibly taken from his hands. When he asked his doctor still again for poison, he killed himself rather than give it.''

Hadrian's death soon followed, due to heart failure, brought on by the disease attacking his legs, or perhaps the result of the abuse of alcohol, used now to decrease his pain, but whose roots began decades before when he went from tavern to tavern with Trajan, both men drinking themselves into a stupor.

Hadrian's successor, Antoninus, saw to Hadrian's funeral pyre and gave the eulogy. Antoninus had to insist on Hadrian's deification because Hadian had made so many enemies in the Senate during his reign, enemies who now gave voice to their former spinelessness.

And now the final question: In the secret of the alcove, in his belovèd's arms, had Hadrian convinced the young and grateful Antinous to sacrifice his beauty and the years left to him so that he, emperor of the civilized world, could live on to do good ... or, more prosaic, so he could simply live on?

SOURCES

(1) See my autobiography *Michael Hone, His World, His Loves*.
(2) See my book *Phallus*.
(3) See my book *SPARTA*.
(4) See my book *Greek Homosexuality*.
(5) An extract from my book *TROY*.
(6) See my book *TROY*.
(7) See my book *Phallus*.
(8) See my book *The History of Orgies*.
(9) See my book *The Sacred Band*.
(10) See my book *Roman Homosexuality*.

The major Greek and Roman sources consulted or used in the writing of this book:

<u>Aelianus</u> was a Roman author and teacher of rhetoric who spoke and wrote in Greek.

<u>Aeschylus</u>, of whom 7 out of perhaps 90 plays have survived. His gravestone celebrated his heroism during the victory against the Persians at Marathon and *not his plays*, proof of the extraordinary importance of Greek survival against the barbarians (sadly, he lost his brother at Marathon). He is said to have been a deeply religious person, dedicated to Zeus. As a boy he worked in a vineyard until Dionysus visited him in a dream and directed him to write plays. One of his plays supposedly divulged too much about the Eleusinian Mysteries and he was nearly stoned to death by the audience. He had to stand trial but pleaded ignorance. He got off when the judges learned of the death of his brother at Marathon and when Aeschylus showed the wounds he and a second brother had received at Marathon too, the second brother left with but a stump in place of his hand. In one of his later plays Pericles was part of the chorus. The subjects of his plays often concerned Troy and the Persian Wars, Marathon, Salamis and Xerxes (Xerxes is accused of losing the war due to hubris; his building of the bridge over the Hellespont was a show of arrogance the gods found unacceptable). In *Seven*

against Thebes he relates the destinies of Oedipus' two sons who agree to become kings of Thebes on alternate years. Naturally, when the time comes for them to change places the king in place refuses, which leads to both boys killing each other. *Agamemnon* is an excellent retelling of the Trojan War, as Agamemnon sails home to be murdered by his wife Clytemnestra. In *The Libation Bearers* Agamemnon's boy Orestes returns home to destroy his father's assassins, Clytemnestra and her lover Aegisthus. In *The Eumenides* (the Kindly Spirits) Orestes is chased by the Furies for having killed his mother. He takes shelter with Apollo who decides, with Athena, to try the boy before a court. The vote is a tie, but Athena, preaching the importance of reason and understanding, acquits him. She then changes the terrible Furies into sweet Eumenides.

Anacreon was born in 582 B.C. and was known for his drinking songs.

Andocides was implicated in the Hermes scandal and saved his skin by turning against Alcibiades in a speech that has come down to us called, what else?, *Against Alcibiades*.

Appian, who lived during the reigns of Trajan and Hadrian, was a Roman historian of Greek origin. He was a friend of Fronto, Marcus Aurelius' tutor and, perhaps, lover. He left his book, *Roman History*, which describes, among other events, the Roman civil wars.

Aristophanes, my preferred playwright, is, naturally, the father of comedy. He wrote perhaps 40 plays of which 11 remain. He was feared by all: Plato states that it was his play *The Clouds* the root of the trial that cost Socrates his life. Nearly nothing is known about him other than what he himself revealed in his works. Playwrights were obliged to be conservative because part of each play was funded by a wealthy citizen, an honor for the citizen and a caveat for the author. He was an exponent of make-love-not-war who saw his country go from its wonderful defeat of the Persians to its end at the hands of the Spartans. Along with Alcibiades and Socrates, Aristophanes is featured in Plato's *The Symposium* in which he is gently mocked, proof that he was considered, even by those he poked fun at, as affable. *The Acharnians* highlights the troubles the Athenians went through after the death of Pericles and their defeat at the hands of Sparta. *The Peace* focuses on the Peace of Nicias. *Lysistrata* tells about the plight of women trying to bring about peace in order to prevent the sacrifice of their sons during war, occasioning the world's first sex strike. When Athens lost its freedom to Sparta, Aristophanes stopped writing plays.

Athenaeus lived in the times of Marcus Aurelius. His *Deipnosopistae* is a banquet conversation *à la Platon* during which conversations on every possible subject takes place, filling fifteen books that have come down to us.

Ausonius was a Latin poet and teacher of rhetoric, around 350 B.C.

Bion was a Greek philosopher known for his diatribes, satires and attacks on religion. He lived around 300 B.C.

Cassius Dio, 155 A.D. to 235 A.D., was a noted historian who wrote in Greek and published a history of Rome in 80 volumes, many of which have survived, giving modern historians a detailed look into his times.

Cicero was born in 106 B.C. and murdered by Marc Antony in 43 B.C. Michael Grant said it all when he wrote, "the influence of Cicero upon the history of European literature and ideas greatly exceeds that of any other prose writer in any language."

Cornelius Nepos was a Roman friend of Cicero. Most of what he wrote was lost, so what we know comes through passages of his works in the books of other historians.

Ctesias was a Greek historian from Anatolian Caria, and the physican of Artaxerxes, whom he accompanied in his war against his brother Cyrus the Younger. He wrote a book on India, *Indica* and Persia, *Persica*. The fragments we have of his writing come to us through Diodorus Siculus and Plutarch.

Diodorus Siculus lived around 50 B.C. and wrote *Historical Library*, consisting of forty volumes.

Diogenes of Sinope (aka Diogenes the Cynic) comes to use through extracts of his writing passed on by others, as nothing he wrote has survived. He had a truly remarkable life, at first imprisoned for debasing the coins his father, a banker, minted. Afterwards he pled poverty, sleeping in a huge ceramic jar, walking the streets of Athens during the day with a lighted lamp, saying he was in search of an honest man, and teasing Plato by noisily eating through his lectures (later Plato claimed he was "a Socrates gone mad"). On a voyage he was captured and sold as a slave in Crete to a Corinthian who was so entranced by his intelligence that he made him his sons' teacher. It was in his master's household that he grew old and died. Plutarch tells us he met Alexander the Great while Diogenes was staring at a pile of bones. In answer to Alexander's question he said he was searching for the bones of Alexander's father, but could not distinguish them from those of a slave. Alexander supposedly said that if he couldn't be Alexander he would choose to be Diogenes. He was the first man ever to claim to be "a citizen of the world." He urinated on people, defecated where he would and masturbated in public, about which he said, "If only I could banish hunger by rubbing my belly." The word cynic meant dog-like, and when someone questioned him about it he said he too was dog-like because he licked those who helped him, barked at those who didn't, and bit his enemies. Rogers and Hart wrote these lyrics about him: There was an old zany/who lived in a tub; he had so many flea-bites/he didn't know where to rub.

<u>Eupolis</u> lived around 430 B.C. An Athenian poet who wrote during the Peloponnesian Wars.

<u>Euripides</u> may have written 90 plays of which 18 survive. His approach was a study of the inner lives of his personages, the predecessor of Shakespeare. Due to his stance on certain subjects, he thought it best to leave Athens voluntarily rather than suffer an end similar to that of Socrates. An example: "I would prefer to stand three times to confront my enemies in battle rather than bear a single child!" He was born on the island of Salamis, of Persian-War fame; in fact he was born on the very day of the battle. His youth was spent in athletics and dance. Due to bad marriages with unfaithful wives, he withdrew to Salamis where he wrote while contemplating sea and sky. When Sparta defeated Athens in war, it did not burn the city to the ground: Plutarch states that this was thanks to one of Euripides' plays, *Electra*, put on for the Spartans in Athens, a play they found so wonderful that they proclaimed that it would be barbarous to destroy a city capable of engendering men of the quality of Euripides. (The real

reason was to preserve the city that had twice saved Greece from Persian victory.) Euripides was known for his love of Agathon, a youth praised for his beauty as well as for his culture, and would later become a playwright. Aristophanes mocked Euripides for loving Agathon long after he had left his boyhood behind him. (Remember, not everyone followed boy-love to the letter. The idea of men loving boys until they grew whiskers did not always hold true. Boys grown "old" could shave their chins and butts; some men just preferred other men, hairy or not, while most men impregnated boys but other men adored being penetrated.) Plato says that Agathon had polished manners, wealth, wisdom and dispensed hospitality with ease and refinement.

<u>Herodian</u> wrote a history of Greece entitled *History of the Empire from the Death of Marcus*, in eight books. Thanks to him we learn a great deal about Elagabalus.

<u>Herodotus</u> was contemporary to some of the events that interest us here. Cicero called him the Father of History, while Plutarch wrote that he was the Father of Lies. His masterpiece is *The Histories*, considered a chef-d'oeuvre, a work that the gods have preserved intact right up to our own day, a divine intervention that would not have surprised a believer like Herodotus (it's also a book I reread every year). Part of his work may have been derived from other sources (what historian's work isn't?) and the facts rearranged in an effort to give them dramatic force and please an audience. Much of what he did was based on oral histories, many of which themselves were based on early folk tales, highly suspect, naturally, in all their details. Aristophanes made fun of segments of his work and Thucydides called Herodotus a storyteller. Surprisingly little is known about his own life. For example, he writes lovingly about Samos, leading some to believe that he may have spent his youth there. Born near Ionia, he wrote in that dialect, learning it perhaps on Samos. He was his own best publicist, taking his works to festivals and games, such as the Olympic Games, and reading them to the spectators. As I've said, many people doubt that he actually went where he said he went and saw what he said he saw. But the same was true of Marco Polo who causes disbelief to this day simply because he never mentioned eating noodles in China or seeing the Great Wall

or even drinking Chinese tea. No historian, then as now, can write a book on ancient occurrences without referring to Herodotus' observations. An amusing example of recent discoveries that give credence to Herodotus is this: Herodotus wrote about a kind of giant ant, the size of a fox, living in India, in the desert, that dug up gold. This was ridiculed until the French ethnologist Peissel came upon a marmot living in today's Pakistan that burrows in the sand and has for generations brought wealth to the region by bringing up gold from its burrows. Peissel suggests that the original confusion came from the fact that the Persian word for marmot was similar to the word for mountain ant.

Historia Augusta. The *Historia Augusta* is a conundrum and a huge historical headache. Modern historians refuse to abandon it because it is the unique source of information concerning 3rd century emperors. It is certainly based on Suetonius' *The Twelve Caesars* and was originally thought to have had six authors, although some historians today believe there was only one, writing somewhere between 350-450 AD. Many historians also believe that its contents--letters, speeches and decrees--are fraudulent.

<u>Isocrate</u> was a student of Socrates who wrote a speech in the defense of Alcibiades during a trial that took place after his death.

<u>Josephus</u>, 37 A.D. to around 100 A.D., was a historian born in Jerusalem. He fought against the Romans and was captured by Vespasian who kept him as his interpreter and, later, Josephus even assumed the emperor's family name, becoming a citizen (Titus Flavius Josephus). A Jew, he turned against his people and helped Vespasian's son Titus to loot the Second Temple. His works include *The Jewish War* and *Antiquities of the Jews.*

<u>Juvenal</u> was a satirical poet who wrote *Satires*.

<u>Lucan</u> (Marcus Annaeus Lucanus) lived from 39 A.D. to 65 A.D., a short life due to his being ordered by Nero to commit suicide because of his role in the treasonous Piso conspiracy. In hopes of a pardon, he implicated his mother among others, all of whom followed him in death. He was a poet, a close friend of Nero until the emperor grew tired of him and his poetry, after which Lucan's writing became insulting, insults Nero was said to have ignored.

Lysias was extremely wealthy and contemporary with Alcibiades. He founded a new profession, logographer, which consisted of writing speeches delivered in law courts. One of his speeches was *Against Andocides*, another was *Against Alcibiades*.

Memmius was an orator and poet, and friend of Pompey but eventually went over to Caesar.

Mimnermus was born in Ionian Smyrna around 630 B.C. He wrote short love poems suitable for performance at drinking parties.

Myron of Priene is the author of a historical account of the First Messenian War.

Pausanias, a Greek historian and geographer, famous for his *Description of Greece*. He was contemporary with Hadrian and Marcus Aurelius. He's noted as being someone interested in everything, careful in his writing and scrupulously honest.

Phanocles lived during the time of Alexander the Great. He was the author of a poem on boy-love that described the love of Orpheus for Calais, and his death at the hands of Thracian women.

Philemon lived to be a hundred but alas only fragments of his works remain. He must have been very popular as he won numerous victories as a poet and playwright.

Pindar's great love was Theoxenus of Tenodos about whom he wrote: ''Whosoever, once he has seen the rays flashing from the eyes of Theoxenus, and is not shattered by the waves of desire, has a black heart forged of a cold flame. Like wax of the sacred bees, I melt when I look at the young limbs of boys.'' He lived around 500 B.C. and celebrated the Greek victories against the Persians at Salamis and Plataea. His home in Thebes became a must for his devotees.

Plato was a major source for this book, along with Xenophon, Thucydides and Plutarch. Plato's most famous work is the Allegory of the Cave. Humans in the cave have no other reality than the shadows they see on the walls. If they looked around, they could see what was casting the shadows and by doing so gain additional knowledge. If they left the cave they would discover the sun, analogous to truth. If those who saw the sun reentered the cave and told the others, they would not be believed. There are thusly different levels of reality that only the wisest are able to see; the others remain ignorant. It's basically thanks to Plato and Xenophon that we know what we do about Socrates. Plato's perfect republic is ruled by the best (an aristocracy), headed by a philosopher king who guides his people thanks to his wisdom and reason. An inferior form of government, one that comes after an aristocracy, is a timocracy, ruled by the honorable. A timocracy is in the hands of a warrior class. Plato has Sparta in mind, but it's unclear how he could have found this form of government better than, for example, a democracy. The problem may be that we know, in reality, so little about Sparta. Next comes an oligarchy based on wealth, followed by a democracy, rule by just anyone and everyone. This degenerates into a tyranny, meaning a government of oppression, because of the conflict between the rich and the poor in a democracy.

Pliny the Younger was the Elder's nephew. He witnessed the explosion of Vesuvius. He was a lawyer and a letter writer, many of which remain, vital historical sources of the times. His letters concerning Trajan are of special importance. Under Trajan he worked side by side with Suetonius.

Plutarch was born near Delphi around 46 A.D. to a wealthy family. He was married, and a letter to his wife even exists to this day. He had sons, the exact number unknown. He studied mathematics and philosophy in Athens and was known to have visited most of the major Greek sites mentioned in this book, as well as Rome. He personally knew Emperors Trajan and Hadrian, and became a Roman citizen. He was a high priest at Delphi and his duty consisted of interpreting the auguries of the Pythoness (no mean task). He wrote the *Lives of the Emperors* but alas only two of the lesser emperors survive. Another verily monumental work was *Parallel Lives of Greeks and Romans* of which twenty-three exist. His interest was the destinies of his subjects, how they made their way through the meanders of life, the Jekyll/Hyde struggle of virtue versus vice. A small jest, he went on, often reveals more than battles during which thousands die. His writings on Sparta, alongside those of Xenophon, are nearly all we possess concerning that extraordinary city-state. His major biographies are the *Life of Alexander* and the *Life of Julius*

Caesar. Amusingly, Plutarch wrote a scathing review of Herodotus' work in which he stated that the great historian was fanatically biased in favor of the Greeks who could do, according to Herodotus, no wrong.

No gratitude can ever be enough for what this man has given us, although in the case of the Greeks we must never forget that he was writing *500 years after the events*.

Polybius, around 200 B.C. to 118 B.C., was a Greek historian whose *The Histories* covered the period from 264 to 146 B.C. He was a friend of Scipio Africanus. He details the ascent to empire of Rome, and was present at the destruction of Carthage.

Polyenus was a Macedonian known as a rhetorician and for his books on war strategies.

Sallust was a Roman historian and politician, 86 B.C. to about 35 B.C. One of his works concerned Catiline and he wrote *Histories* of which only fragments remain.

Seneca (Lucius Annaeus Seneca) lived around 4 B.C. to 65 A.D. He was the advisor of Caligula, Claudius and Nero who forced him to commit suicide for supposedly planning his overthrow. He is known for his philosophical essays, letters and tragedies.

Simonides of Ceos was a Greek poet born about 550 B.C. Besides his poems, he added four letters to the Greek alphabet.

Suetonius (Gaius Suetonius Tranquillus) lived around 69 A.D. to 123 A.D. He was a truly great Roman historian known for his *Twelve Caesars*, his only extant work. Pliny the Younger says that he was studious and totally dedicated to writing. He was highly favored by both Trajan, under whom he served as his secretary, and Hadrian who fired him for having an affair with the Empress Vibia Sabina.

Sophocles was the author of 123 plays of which 7 remain, notably *Oedipus* and *Antigone*. An Athenian born to a rich family just before the Battle of Marathon, he was a firm supporter of Pericles. He fought alongside Pericles against Samos when the island attempted to become autonomous from Athens. He was elected as a magistrate during the Sicilian Expedition led by Alcibiades, and given for function the goal of finding out why the expedition had ended disastrously. Sophocles was always ready and willing to succumb to the charms of boys. Plutarch tells us that even at age 65 ''Sophocles led a handsome boy outside the city walls to have his way with him. He spread the boy's poor himation [a rectangular piece of cloth thrown over the left shoulder that drapes the body] upon the ground. To cover them both he spread his rich cloak. After Sophocles took his pleasure the boy took the cloak and left the himation for Sophocles. This misadventure was eventually known to all.'' He died at 90, some say while reciting a very long tirade from *Antigone* because he hadn't paused to take a breath. Another version has him choking on grapes, and a final one has him dying of happiness after winning the equivalent of our Oscar at a festival. The first of his trilogy--called the Theban plays--is *Oedipus the King*. Here the baby Oedipus--in a plot that goes back to Priam and Paris at the founding of Troy--is handed over to a servant to be killed in order to prevent the accomplishment of an oracle, an oracle stating that he will kill his father and marry his mother. He does both after solving the riddle of the sphinx (which creature becomes four-footed, then two-footed and finally three-footed?). His mother, when she finds out she's been bedding her own son, commits suicide and Oedipus blinds himself. In *Oedipus at Colonus* Oedipus dies and we learn more about his children Antigone, Polyneices and Eteocles. In *Antigone* Polyneices is accused of treason and killed. His body is thrown outside the city walls and the king forbids its burial, under pain of death. Antigone does so anyway and, faced with death, she commits suicide, followed by the king's son who was going to wed her, followed by the king's wife who couldn't face losing her precious son (Whew!).

<u>Tacitus</u>, around 56 A.D. to 117 A.D., was a historian who wrote *Annals* and *Histories*, concerning Tiberius, Claudius, Nero and the Year of the Four Emperors. He is known for his insights into the psychology of his subjects.

<u>Theocritus</u> was a Sicilian and lived around 270 B.C. In his 7th Idyll Aratus is passionately in love with a lad. His 12th Idyll refers to Diocles who died saving the life of Philolaus, the boy he loved, and in whose honor kissing contests were held every spring at his tomb. In his 23rd Idyll a lover commits suicide because of unrequited love, warning his belovèd that one day he too will burn

and weep for a cruel boy. Before hanging himself the lover kissed the doorpost from which he would attach the noose. The boy treated the corpse with disdain and went off to the gymnasium for a swim where a statue of Eros fell on him, coloring the water with his blood. In his 29th Idyll a lover warns his belovèd that he too will age and his beauty will lose its freshness. He is therefore advised to show more kindness as "you will one day be desperate for a beautiful young man's attentions." Although lads are often disappointing, it is impossible not to fall madly in love with them. In the 30th Idyll the poet states that when a man grows old he should keep a distance from boys, but in his heart he knows that the only alternative to loving a boy is simply to cease to exist.

<u>Theognis</u> was born around 550 B.C. His poems consist of maxims and advice as to how to live life. Fortunately, a great deal of his work has come down to us, most of which is dedicated to his belovèd, the handsome Cyrnus.

<u>Thucydides</u> was an Athenian general and historian, contemporary with the events he described. What he wrote was based on what actually happened; there was no extrapolating; no divine intervention on the part of the gods as was the case with Plutarch. An example of this was his observation that birds and animals which ate plague victims died as a result, leading him to conclude that the disease had a natural rather than supernatural cause. His description of the plague has never been equaled, the plague that he himself caught while participating in the Peloponnesian War. He is thought to have died in 411 B.C., the date at which his writing suddenly stops. He admired Pericles and democracy but not the radical form found in Athens.

<u>Tyrtaeus</u>, a rare Spartan writer, left us an account of the Second Messenian War. The purpose of his poetry was to inspire Spartan support of the Spartan state. Athenians claimed he was of Athenian birth. Pausanias maintained that the Athenians had sent him to Sparta as an insult, because he was both crazy, lame and had one eye. Herodotus wrote that he was only one of two foreigners to be given Spartan citizenship.

<u>Xenophon</u>, born near Athens in 430 B.C., was a historian and general. His masterpieces are *The Peloponnesian Wars* and *Anabasis.* He loved Sparta and served under Spartan generals

during the Persian Wars. Like the Spartans, he believed in oligarchic rule, rule by the few, be they the most intelligent or wealthy or militarily acute. He spent a great deal of time in Persia alongside Cyrus the Younger who raised an army, among whom were Xenophon's 10,000 and other mercenaries (all of which is the subject of *Anabasis*). After Cyrus' death Xenophon and his ten thousand made their way back home, the breathtaking account of which ends his *Anabasis*. The Athenians exiled him when he fought with the Spartans against Athens but the Spartans offered him an estate where he wrote his works. His banishment may have been revoked thanks to his son Gryllus who brilliantly fought and died for Athens.

Other Sources

Abbott Jacob, *History of Pyrrhus*, 2009
Aldrich, Robert, *Who's Who in Gay and Lesbian History*, 2001.
Aristophanes, Bantam Drama, 1962.
Baker Simon, *Ancient Rome*, 2006
Barber, Stanley, *Alexandros*, 2010.
Bury and Meiggs, *A History of Greece*, 1975.
Calimach, Andrew, *Lover's Legends*, 2002.
Ceram, C.W., *Gods, Graves and Scholars*, 1951.
Davidson, James, *Courtesans and Fishcakes*, 1998.
Davidson, James, *The Greeks and Greek Love*, 2007.
Dover K.J. *Greek Homosexuality*, 1978
Everitt Anthony, *Augustus*, 2006
Everitt Anthony, *Cicero*, 2001
Everitt Anthony, *Hadrian*, 2009
Fagles, Robert, *The Iliad*, 1990
Goldsworthy Adrian, *Caesar*, 2006
Goldsworthy Adrian, *The Fall of Carthage*, 2000
Goodman Rob and Soni Jimmy, *Rome's Last Citizen*, 2012
Grant Michael, *History of Rome*, 1978
Graves, Robert, *Greek Myths*, 1955
Halperin David M. *One Hundred Years of Homosexuality*, 1990
Harris Robert, *Imperium*, 2006
Herodotus, *The Histories*, Penguin Classics.

Hesiod and Theognis, Penguin Classics, 1973
Hine, Daryl, *Puerilities*, 2001
Holland Tom, *Rubicon*, 2003
Hughes Robert, *Rome*, 2011
Hughes-Hallett, *Heroes*, 2004
Lévy, *Edmond, Sparte, 1979*
Livy, *Rome and the Mediterranean*
Livy, *The War with Hannibal*
Malye, Jean, *La Véritable Histore d'Alcibiade*, 2009
Matyszak Philip, *Mithridates the Great*, 2008
McLynn, *Marcus Aurelius*, 2009
Meyer, Jack, *Alcibiades*, 2009
Miles Richard, *Ancient Worlds*, 2010
Miles Richard, *Carthage Must be Destroyed*, 2010
Morwood, James, *Hadrian*, 2013
Opper, Thorsten, *Hadrian, Empire and Conflict*, 2008.
Peyrefitte, Roger, *Alexandre*, 1979.
Plutarch's Lives, Modern Library.
Polybius, *The Histories*
Renucci Pierre, *Caligula*, 2000
Romans Grecs et Latin, Gallimard, 1958
Rouse, W.H.D., Homer's *The Iliad*, 1938
Schiff, Stacy, *Cleopatra*, 2010
Southern, P. *The Roman Army, a Social and Institutional History*
Strauss Barry, *The Spartacus War*, 2009
Suetonius, *The Twelve Caesars*
Tacitus, *The Annals of Imperial Rome*
Tacitus, *The Histories*
Thucydides, *The Peloponnesian War*, Penguin Classics
Tibullus, *The Elegies of Tibullus*, by Theodore C. Williams
Vernant, Jean-Pierre, *Mortals and Immortals*, 1991
Virgil, *The Aeneid*, Everyman's Library, Knopf, 1907
Ward-Perkins Bryan, *The Fall of Rome*, 2005
Wheaton James, *Spartacus*, 2011
Wikipedia: Research today is impossible without this monument
Williams Craig A. *Roman Homosexuality*, 2010
Williams John, *Augustus*, 1972
Xenophon, *A History of My Times*, Penguin Classics

Xenophon, *The Persian Expedition*, 1949

INDEX

Please note that the page numbers are *passim*. An example, Tiberius 76 – 102 means that Tiberius is found within these pages, but not necessarily on *every* page.

Academy 63-68
Achilles 68-86, 91-101
Aelius, Lucius 107-112
Aemilianus, Scipio 31-40
Aeneas 7-16, 31-40, 101-107
Afer, Publius Aelius Hadrianus *passim*
Africanus, Scipio 31-40
Aias 91-101
Alcibiades 49-56
Alexamenos 56-63
Alexander 16-31
Alexander the Great 16-31, 49-56, 68-86, 91-101
Anabasis 16-31
Antinous *passim*
Antonius Pius 107-112
Antony 101-107
Antony, Marc 40-49, 56-63, 68-86
Aphrodite 101-107
Apollo *passim*
Apology 16-31
Aristogeiton 68-86
Assassins 91-101
Athenaeus of Naucratis 63-68
Attalus 68-86
Augustus, Emperor 7-16, 40-49
Aurelius, Marcus 86-91, 107-112
Author Tudor 7-16
Baal 68-86
Bacchus 7-16
Barca, Hamilcar 31-40
Batavian Guard 40-49
Board of Ten 7-16
Bret, David 68-86

Caesar, Julius *passim*
Caligula 40-49, 63-68, 91-101
Caracalla, Emperor 68-86, 107-112
Cassius Dio 91-101
Catherine of Aragon 7-16
Cato 31-40
Cicero 40-49
Circus Maximus 16-31
Circus Maximus 40-49
Claudius, Emperor 7-16
Cleopatra 101-107
Cline, Walter 56-63
Commodus, Emperor 107-112
Crassus, Marcus Licinius 40-49
Curio, Gaius 68-86
Curtis, Tony 49-56
Cynics 91-101
Cyrus the Younger 16-31
Dacian Wars 16-31, 40-49
Daphne 101-107
Darius 16-31
David 91-101
Davidson, James 7-16
Decebalus 16-31
Delphi 68-86
Dido, Queen 31-40
Dio, Cassius 91-101
Diogenes the Cynic 49-56
Diomedes 101-107
Dionysus 7-16, 86-91
Domitian 16-31
Domitian, Emperor 7-16, 16-31
Eburnus, Quintus Fabius Maximus 16-31
El-Gabal 68-86
Elagaballium (Marcus Aurelius Antoninus Augustus) 68-86
Elagabalus 68-86
Ennius, Quintus 31-40
Epaminondas 101-107
Epictetus 86-91
Epicurean 86-91
Epicureanism 7-16
Epicurus 7-16, 86-91
Episthenes 16-31

Eros 7-16, 68-86
Errol Flynn 68-86
Etruscans sexuality 63-68
Euphrates 86-91
Fabio, Julius 107-112
Faustina 107-112
Fellini 7-16
First Punic War 7-16, 31-40
Five Good Emperors 107-112
Flynn, Errol 68-86
Fuscus 112-115
Ganymede 68-86, 101-107
Germana 7-16, 63-68
Hadrian, Emperor *passim*
Hadrian's Wall 40-49
Hadrianopolis 101-107
Hamilcar 31-40
Hannibal Barca 31-40
Hanno 31-40
Harmodius 68-86
Hasdrubal 31-40
Helen of Sparta 56-63, 91-101
Helios 101-107
Hellenica 16-31
Henry VIII 7-16
Hephaestion 91-101
Hera 86-91
Heracles 49-56
Hermes 49-56, 68-86
Hermogenes 112-115
Hierocles 68-86
Hipparchus 68-86
Horoscopes 86-91
Hyacinth 7-16, 101-107
Incitatus 91-101
Ippias 68-86
Isis 63-68, 86-91
Kokhba, Bar 101-107
Kurnos 49-56
Lemmon, Jack 49-56
Liber Lares 7-16
Longinus, Cnaeus Pompeius 16-31
Longus, Tiberius Sempronius 31-40

Lucilla, Annia 107-112
Lucius Verus 49-56
Lyceum 63-68
Lycurgus 68-86
Lysander 16-31
Machiavelli, Niccolò 107-112
Maesa, Julia 68-86
Magna Graecia 31-40
Mago 31-40
Marsyas 68-86
Martialis, Julius 68-86
Masada 101-107
Mastor 112-115
Maugham, Robin 56-63
Menelaus 91-101
Metelus 31-40
Michelangelo 91-101
Mithridates 16-31, 40-49
Myrmidons 91-101
Nero 40-49, 68-86. 86-91, 101-107
Nerva, Emperor 16-31
Nestor 68-86
Nestor 91-101
Nicomedes, King 16-31, 49-56, 68-86
On Famous Men 40-49
Osirantinous 91-101
Osiris 63-68, 86-91, 91-101
Pachrates 16-31, 91-101
Paedogogum 56-63
Pantheon 40-49
Paris 91-101
Paris, Prince of Troy 56-63, 91-101
Patroclus 91-101
Pausanias 68-86
Philip of Macedon 68-86
Plato 16-31, 68-86
Pliny the Younger 16-31
Plotina 16-31, 86-91
Poikile 63-68
Pompey the Great 40-49, 101-107
Postumus 40-49
Praetorian Guard 40-49
Proscriptions 40-49

Prytaneum 63-68
Ptolemy I 63-68
Pualina, Domitia 7-16
Pylandes 16-31
Pyrrhus 31-40
Quintianus 107-112
Rhea 86-91
Richard I Cœur de Lion 91-101, 112-115
Sabina, Vibia 16-31, 63-68
Sabinus II, Titus Flavius 16-31
Sacred Band 68-86, 101-107
Saladin 91-101
Salinder, Gnaeus Pedanius Fuscus 16-31
Saurus 49-56
Scaurus, Quintus Terentius 7-16
Scipio Africanus 31-40
Second Punic War 31-40
Second Triumvirate 40-49
Servianus, Lucius 112-115
Set 86-91
Seuthes 16-31
Severus, Julius 101-107
Sicarii 101-107
Sinan 91-101
Siwa 91-101
Siwa, Oracle of 56-63, 91-101
Socrates 49-56
Some Like It Hot 49-56
Steindorff, George v
Stephanus 16-31
Stoicism 7-16
Stoics 40-49, 86-91, 107-112
Stone, Oliver 16-31
Suetonius 16-31, 40-49
Sulla 16-31
Symposium 68-86
Teiresias 68-86
Teucer 91-101
The Lives of the Caesars 40-49
The Sacred Band 49-56
Theopompus 63-68
Tiberius 40-49
Tibullus 49-56

Tibur 63-68, 91-101
Timaleus 49-56
Titus, Emperor 7-16, 16-31, 101-107
Tivoli 63-68
Toga praetexta 7-16
Toga virilis 7-16
Trajan, Emperor *passim*
Verus, Lucius 107-112
Verus, Lucius 49-56
Vespasian, Emperor 7-16, 16-31, 101-107
Victor, Aurelius 91-101
Xanthippus 31-40
Xenophon 16-31, 68-86, 101-107
Zealots 101-107
Zeus *passim*
Zoticus, Aurelius 68-86

Printed in Great Britain
by Amazon